THE LINDEMANN THEORY

A 31 YEAR JOURNEY AND MY CURE

For the
Professional

Robert Lindemann

RWL
CONSULTING
LLC

Robert Lindemann/RWL Consulting LLC
www.TheLindemannTheory.com
Printed in the United States of America

The Lindemann Theory/ Robert Lindemann -- 1st ed.

ISBN 978-0-9996680-0-9 Print Edition

ISBN 978-0-9996680-1-6 Ebook Edition

Library of Congress Control Number: 2017964754

CONTENTS

nine years—that the science behind ideas presented in this book, and the analysis of his case history, constitute a cure. This is due to the author's opinion, with strong scientific backing: many adverse symptoms, side effects and created sequela in his case history were created by the very medications he was taking for the parent disorder.

Two version of the *Lindemann Theory, A 31 Year Journey and My Cure* have been created. The version denoted *For the World*, is a softer version in regards to the science and medical terminology used. The version, *For the Professional* goes into a bit more depth and detail, using more medical terms and descriptions.

The concepts and theories in both are the same. The *For the World* reader, can always expand the breadth of their knowledge and graduate to the Pro version – enjoy!

A Letter to my Reader

Dear Reader,

When was the last time you took notice of young toddlers at play and witnessed the joy, love, innocence, fire for learning, void of inhibition and infinite energy they exude: a sight that just left you chuckling with a friend?

Or when was the last time you laid down on a forest floor on a cool summer's eve and listened to the canopy's opera of chattering birds, just prior to the silence that ensues when the sun finally sets, and nature grants permission to rest?

We're a species that certainly "enjoys" different viewpoints and manufacturers opinions—usually too quickly and in abundance— but I believe we all can agree our time on this rotating sphere we call home is finite. I can only hope after this read, you learn to live in the moment and enjoy this gift of life.

I can only hope you do not have to learn this lesson the hard way, as I did. I wish to find the courage to share with you a story, and open my heart, so my words flow smoothly and inspire, teach and drive your thirst for more knowledge, and for more in life.

There is nothing wrong, yet everything right and wonderful with hope.

Wishing us all the best, with gratitude,

Robert W. Lindemann

Truth Be Told

The lifetime risk of suicide for human beings who have suffered untreated depressive disorder is close to 20%. For ages fifteen through twenty-four, suicide rates have increased more than 200% in the last fifty years.

These figures are alarming numbers, considering a study in 2008 reports an estimated 9% of the U.S. population suffer from some form of depression, while 3.4% suffer from major depression. Economically, the cost of depressive illness hits thirty to forty-four billion dollars per year for the U.S. alone. Depression is considered the second-leading cause of disability worldwide.

Depression is but one form of mental illness. All mental illnesses combined leave one out of every four—yes, 25%—of Americans per year suffering. One in seventeen (13.6 million) suffer with more serious illnesses such as schizophrenia, major depression or bipolar depression. In totality, the economic costs of serious mental illnesses hit $193 billion per year.

It is my opinion that discussing suicide does not lead to either suicidal ideation or suicide. In fact, I believe talking about suicide can save countless lives! Confronting one's fears can set one free.

On April 2, 2013, the White House announced the Brain Initiative, a research endeavor that set a goal to revolutionize man's understanding of the human mind and uncover new ways to treat, prevent and cure brain disorders like Alzheimer's, schizophrenia, autism, obsessive-compulsive disorder (OCD), depression and traumatic brain injury. This program should be greeted with warmth, not only because of the above heart-wrenching statistics, but because of the program's promise, given by the Human Genome Project: $3.8 billion invested and $796 billion generated back ($141 back for every dollar put in).

I hope this book might be a small part of that revolution, as the concepts and excitement for The Lindemann Theory and InfinitE/IQ become elucidated.

There is nothing wrong, but everything right with hope!

Robert W. Lindemann

Introduction

The conversation on that fall day in 2013 was brief, but intriguing and inspiring. The phone call proceeded as follows:

"Robert, I wanted to thank you for our conversation last night. I simply never understood. Thank you."

I replied, "You are very, very welcome." I felt I had comforted and taught someone, and given them peace.

The "thank you" was said with such sincere, refreshing gratitude I was pushed back to what I already knew I wanted to do. The wheels in my mind started turning.

I remember the night of that conversation vividly. Certainly, it never would have happened, had not a head cold clogged my ears and nose, rendering me tired and vulnerable. My young beautiful one and two-year olds' nightly alarms had also rendered entrance to deep sleep a near impossibility for weeks prior, again leaving me—well—frankly, brain numb.

Ted, a very good friend, was in from Chicago on business. We met and had dinner at another friend's restaurant, *Rapture*. Dan sat down with Ted and me, and his waiters presented us with a wonderful bottle of merlot. A banquet was to follow. Certainly, we spoke of the glory days, after a chat of twenty-first century politics, economics and world current events left us stranded in the "glass-half-empty mentality"—rather than the fuller bouquet of the topped-off merlot.

It was during the glass-half-empty stage of the conversation when

Dan spoke of a friend, who had thrown himself in front of a train, ending his life. He left many, including himself, quite effected—actually devastated. It was when Dan stated, "How could he have been such a coward!" that I knew immediately the truth needed to follow; the truth to set the three of us, and countless others, free.

I knew the truth, because I lived and experienced it. I was thankful my two friends had not experienced it. I do not want any of you to experience it, either.

I first explained a lecture I had sat through during my collegiate studies. The class was Psychology 101, a class which usually is the standard course to present the controversial work of Dr. Harry Harlow from the 1950s to 1960s. His work was controversial because he performed experiments on juvenile Rhesus macaques, a social animal like humans, whereby he subjected them to social isolation to create a model for the study of depression. Unfortunately, it was a very successful model. Indeed, the depth of the depression experienced by these primates was so severe many of them starved themselves to death. I recall the professor even saying one monkey actually hung himself, although I was unable to verify this through reviewing Harlow's writings or available research.

I took a deep breath and explained to Ted and Dan I had also experienced such a plunge into darkness. It was a place filled with agonizing mental pain, and was one step further removed from the horribly painful state of severe depression I had already been in. It was a place with no mental consideration of writing a suicide note, but rather an inexplicable drive to end that mental pain through ending my life. "Cowardly?" you say. Folks, I didn't even know what hit me! Remember, man's greatest fear is death. No one rushes to get there!

I want to tell you about that plunging night. I also want to tell you about my thirty-one-year battle with mental illness. It was an illness that manifested at age fifteen with a severe obsessional neurosis, also known as obsessive-compulsive disorder (OCD). *Stedman's Medical Dictionary* defines obsessive compulsive as having the tendency to perform certain repetitive acts or ritualistic behavior to relieve anxiety, as in obsessive-compulsive neurosis. It is a definition, along with others I have seen, that I hope to expand upon and improve. The disorder left me in agonizing pain!

In this memoir, *The Lindemann Theory,* I theorize and believe I can validate an eight-year cure, thus far. The medications that previously removed symptoms of OCD went on to create a broad range of events, including direct side effects, a misdiagnosis and—indirectly—other sequela (conditions following the original disorder of OCD). Eight years ago, in 2009, I would perform a retrospective analysis of these events, leading me to create *The Lindemann Theory*—which would lead to my cure. I went on to create *InfinitE/IQ* to help us all. In this book, the following list of events will be examined in detail. The very events that tortured me would create a history that would set me free.

<u>Events</u>:
- Three major periods of OCD
- Four major depressions
- Three of the major depressions requiring electroconvulsive treatments (ECT)
- Ten to fifteen major "burn-outs" (at least three to six weeks long)
- Two total hallucinatory to full-psychosis events
- Periods of mania, delusions, paranoia, obvious stress and anxiety
- Two lock downs

- Two suicide attempts (one near death)
- Six major hospitalizations (one week or longer)
- Five emergency room visits, thousands of doctor visits
- Twenty direct and one hundred indirect doctors
- Almost twenty different medications
- One sleep research facility experience
- And more

As you can see from the above, I experienced and can understand a vast array of psychiatric conditions. I believe I have an uncommon insight, covering not only symptomatology, but many of the therapeutic modalities available in psychiatric treatment today. Experience, coupled with academia—and driven by empathy and passion—forms the basis for this write and your read.

I have been healthy, happy, symptom free (none, zero), and long-term psychotropic medication and long-term therapy free for the past eight-plus years. My diagnosis today is happy and healthy, and I will explain how this is possible and how it happened.

I simply never want any of you to ever enter that plunge—nor even get close! The restaurant I sat in that night was called *Rapture*: "passion" in French. I have no choice but to write the following pages with passion and joy, from deep in my heart.

Now, while I write with joy and passion, I am also filled with anger. That is OK though, as anger and passion are often needed to wake people up. They are the fire for change. How is it possible we are in the twenty-first century, and there is still a stigma associated with mental illness? It is simply beyond me. We have the knowledge to send a rover laboratory to crawl around on a planet thirty-five-million-miles away, yet we remain naive in calling a suicide victim a coward. We must become educated! The "innocence" of arrogance and ignorance can no longer be acceptable.

It is very simple. Until the words "mental illness" roll off the tongue, drawing the same level of compassion and urgency as the word "cancer", people will continue to needlessly suffer, and yes, die—and research will be stymied.

I am imploring you to listen to my story, my words and my reasons. There is no reason for any of you to ever see the darkness I saw, but every reason to live this life in the moment with joy. I am so humbled, excited and full of gratitude as you move forward in this read.

There is nothing wrong, but everything right with hope!

Robert W. Lindemann

CHAPTER 1

THE TREE OF LIFE

I arrived at the Belle Mead New Jersey Mental Health Facility in the morning, in early July of 2014. I was there to re-visit and interview staff members of the Electroconvulsive Therapy Unit. The ride on familiar roads to the facility was—in itself—a strong enough trigger to jar tears from my eyes. The absence of my father, lost to cancer in 2011, was enough to sustain the flow; he often drove me there.

As I emerged from my vehicle and gazed across the field, I came across a row of trees, nestled parallel to the base of the Sourland Mountain Preserve. I was trying to locate the tree that saved my life. I was looking for the gap in branches that prevented an ascent that surely would have ended my life. It would have prevented me from ever kissing my beautiful wife and wonderful two toddler daughters every dawn of every day: a frenetic climb that would have prevented me from ever finding me—the person who had disappeared since the age of fifteen. A person lost for thirty-one years.

As my eyes honed onto a massive, sprawling oak as a very plausible candidate, that night came racing back in vivid horrific detail. I am going to tell you about that night fifteen years ago, but I beg of you if you can, never let such a night happen to you. I beg of you!

There is nothing wrong, but everything right with hope!

CHAPTER 2

THE PLUNGE

The depression I was in was a deep one. I knew it. It had happened before. And I knew where the horrific depth could lead to, as that had happened once before—back in 1984.

My father often explained to me, the subject of history was always taught the wrong way. Taught with an abundance of dates, facts, figures, names, places and strategies; voluminous words, sentences, paragraphs and pages—but more often than not—void of the lessons learned. I always loved the saying, "I don't make the same mistake twice. Three or four times—but never twice." Humored by it, yes: an advocate of it, no. I understand the value of history: immerse yourself in the study of it and learn from other's oversights and blunders, as well as one's own mistakes.

The call was made to the mental-health facility. I was en route to the Belle Mead, New Jersey 100-plus acre clinic's campus that had helped me on three previous occasions, since the early '80s. Admission information was taken. I was warmly guided, and began my walk to my hall and room. The familiar dining hall was to my right. I then passed the library, chapel and small billiards room to my left, and was on the home stretch to my dedicated hall and room. There was something very different about the walk this time though. It was a difference that would only send me deeper into depression.

The halls were void of people. Void of patients, staff, and the hustle and bustle of the mental health community I was used to in my previous stays—a community that serves to take the mental patient out of the isolating environment perpetuated by the disease of mental illness in the first place. The Harlow monkeys were always in the back of my mind.

So yes, and an absolute yes. There is no question in my mind the treatment of mental illness requires exposure to people, places and things. Human beings are social creatures. Mental illness drives the human being to isolation. Isolation creates stress, stress upon the pituitary-adrenal-cortical system—a system where homeostasis is crucial in allowing brain neurotransmitter levels to remain healthy. No one explained this to the managed-care "architects" of the late 1980s; changes in design resulted in a less stimulating and prosperous environment for the mental health patient.

While managed care put a dent in the numbers of mental health professionals at the clinic and across the country, it by no means affected the warmth and quality of the personnel at the facility.

I explained my depression. I was forty years old and had spent sixteen years studying: first at a major and prestigious New Jersey State University, followed by a major and prestigious Illinois medical school—only to come up empty-handed: no MD. My tenure of schooling was interrupted at the time by inexplicable burnouts, depressions, psychoses, misdiagnoses and non-diagnoses, all of which interrupted my studies and forced me to withdraw from semesters on at least five occasions.

I told myself I was alive and should be thankful. I told myself to pretend there were more people in the halls, more people to talk with. The fact it was Christmas time, a beautiful time of year, did not matter. I told myself I should feel blessed to be alive. So what if there was no MD to my name? So what if I had wasted time and money, and studied unrelentingly at my desk for sixteen years—for naught? It shouldn't be a big deal. I kept telling myself more and more and more things, but the darkness kept growing and growing and growing—as did the fear of the darkness.

The stream of thoughts turned into a river, and the river started to empty into an ocean—and I was going to be swallowed by that ocean, for sure. The harder I tried to swallow the past, the reel of years past became more vivid. I knew I was in trouble. I just knew it. As I write these words, my head is starting to spin right back to that time.

I must stop and tell you lastly, the fear and intuition of knowing—in itself—kept filling the ocean even more. A tidal wave was imminent.

Open your heart, son, and let your emotions paint the pages with words of passion!

CHAPTER 3

DEMONIC WALK INTO THE NIGHT

The mental pain and agony I experienced that night at the clinic was like nothing I had ever felt. I absolutely did not think anything could have matched the mental pain of the obsessions I had experienced in the '80s, nor the deep depression I experienced in 1991—events that dwarfed any sort of physical pain I had experienced during my lifetime. The experience this night had the added component of simply darkness, horror. It even possessed some sort of hellish or demonic component to it.

I simply had to go to staff and say, "Hey, guys and gals, I'm beyond suicidal. Take me to the Acute Care Unit (ACU), sedate me, wake me up in the morning and start an electroconvulsive therapy (ECT) series—ASAP!"

It was a treatment that saved my life before. I knew it worked and had faith it would work again.

There was a force or drive at work, devoid of reason. There simply was no thought component other than flight. I needed out of the facility. I needed to escape!

I stealthily walked to the first door at the end of my hall. I looked left, right, forward and backward, then went out the door. It was nighttime. The patio café was closed, and my furtive footsteps carried me past the café. The chapel was next. I passed the pool room, and then resumed a casual pace past the dining hall. My goal was the admission doors, and the night-time sky. I was but 100 feet away. No plan, just a horror-filled, driving force, wanting ... I simply did not know at this point what the wanting was. I saw the doors. I opened them, and was outside.

Dressed in sneakers, blue jeans and a tee shirt, I entered a most wonderful snowstorm and freezing temperatures. It was December, Christmas time, snowing and cold—my absolute favorite time of year—and, to my wife's dismay, my favorite conditions. It would have simply been a gorgeous, wondrous night under any other circumstances.

The word wondrous is often coupled with a miracle, but there by no means was any heavenly or divine intervention in sight. I had stopped asking for it, anyway. Certainly, a natural inability to comprehend how a Maker could allow such levels of pain had stymied my faith for quite some time. With that said, even as a man of science, I recognized many a man's arrogance and lack of humility has driven them to the big bang and atheistic philosophy. But I simply will always ask, "Why am I here? Why are any of us here? Why I am compelled to help my fellow man, if we survive without purpose?"

Still no plan, rhyme or reason, I began my walk out of the 100-acre campus. I walked slowly, feeling the snow landing gently on my arms, touching my face and covering my hair. I was a walking paradox. It was a walking aura of fear and dread, gliding through a holy night of peace and beauty. White flakes floated about—would my ashes be defying gravity soon?

The medication that rescued me from a depression in the spring of 1992 was losing the battle this ugly evening. Introduced to the United States in 1989, the medication inhibits the reuptake of both dopamine and norepinephrine (NE), leaving increased levels of these neurotransmitters in the space (synapse) between neurons (brain cells). The increased levels of the brain chemicals provide a feedback mechanism, which decreases neuronal firing. Oddly enough, in 1992, the exact mechanism of why this medication worked was little understood. Today, it is more generally accepted the drug works (pharmacodynamics)—though not exclusively—by increasing brain-derived neurotrophic factor and increasing hippocampal neurogenesis. The hippocampus is a structure in the brain involved with emotion, memory and the autonomic nervous center. This pharmacodynamics theory is supported, in part, by the fact the antidepressant effect often takes days or weeks to activate. I will share my own experience with this drug a bit later.

As I walked, I could only imagine the three areas of the brain principally affected by depression: my hippocampus, thalamus and amygdala were in "fireworks-finale mode gone wrong". A firing squad of neuronal chaos drove me past the campus swimming pool, further into the night and on a circuitous route around the facility, towards the woods at the base of the Sourland Mountains.

Walking adjacent to the ECT parking lot, I crossed the road, traversing the rear of the facility, and entered the snow-covered field—my only barrier to nowhere. It was maybe 300 feet to a line of trees that marked the foothills of the mountains. What better time to go mountain climbing, I guess?

I reached the end of the field and entered a thicket of bushes not visible from the road. The mountain was not my intent. I was looking vertical though, alright. The freezing temperatures sufficed as an anesthetic, as thorns pierced my skin and blood spattered my shirt. My pace quickened, and I simply barreled through the thorny barrier with even more purpose. The rush, and uncontrollable hysteria, sent me to the base of a tree.

I began to climb—forearms ripping against bark, frozen fingers grappling branches. I was ten feet up, then fifteen, then twenty and then thirty. It was a quick thirty feet, and I wanted to go higher. My purpose had become clearer. No doubt: I sought freefall. I sought death.

Incredibly, the gap between my thirty-foot branch and the next was at least eight feet. The girth of the tree would not allow me to shimmy up. I was rabid, alright, but did not have the claws needed by an enraged beast to ascend further. I settled on the branch and looked down. My analysis began!

I knew I was already trapped in my brain. But a trapped mind *and* a trapped body, I thought? This seemed incomprehensible, but it was where I was at. Leaping was absolutely not going to be a problem. In some bizarre moment, at thirty feet, I came to understand the Harlow Rhesus monkeys' state of mind: a drive to end it all.

But, I wondered if this drive was strong enough to be maintained during the seconds on the flight down? Surely to die, I would need to impact like a torpedo. Would the human instinct to survive send my neck to the side? Death at thirty feet was not likely, but paralysis, unconsciousness and amputation were probable. I was in no-man's land with freezing temperature and falling snow—frostbite was inevitable. By the time the dogs reached me, amputation seemed likely. The analysis continued, and my cerebral cortex rapidly processed for a solution.

And yes, in some bizarre twist of fate, miracle or migration of thought out of the cerebrum, hippocampus, thalamus and amygdala, my analysis re-wired my neurons. The rush began to subside. I cannot explain it, but the gap in that tree would serve as my life preserver. The rabid beast was yielding, and I started to feel the mental and physical exhaustion, numbness, and the pain of ripped skin across my body. The rush had subsided, and I began to descend.

No release of emotion. No tears. At the bottom of the tree, I picked thorns out of my arms. I walked right back into that same thicket and out into the field: a walk back to the people who could and would save my life with electroconvulsive therapy in the weeks to come.

As I walked across the field, I started to remember what life was like before the nightmare of obsessions hit at age fifteen. I started to remember my childhood before age fifteen: a period of joy, activity and friendships.

I entered the same door I had exited. I found my numb and blood-ied body sitting in a chair, and I remember a male body hugging me and crying uncontrollably. I believe it was one of my brothers, but I never saw a face. That is all I remember!

A sedative injection? A physical collapse? I don't know. The night was over. I would breathe and live again.

There is nothing wrong, but everything right with hope!

CHAPTER 4

BLISS, CHAOS, CUTS AND BRUISES

It was the fall of 1962 when my parents bought me home from the hospital, and I was greeted by two newly-recovered chicken-pox-laden brothers. My lessons in immunology began. I settled in as a newborn in the crib on Winthrop Road of Franklin Township, in Somerset County, New Jersey.

Those places, my home, are mired in history: the *Winthrop* families brought their surname to the New World, as they sought a new life and escape from the political and religious mayhem of the seventeenth century. The colonies emerged, independence was sought and great America leaders were born. Benjamin Franklin managed to have four Franklin Townships in New Jersey named after him, apparently fitting, as the gentleman simply redefined "Jack of all Trades" to "Genius of all Trades". Somerset was the county of rolling hills in England, and New Jersey—of course—one of the original thirteen colonies.

The '60s started off with high promise as John F. Kennedy had big dreams. But his big dreams were met by a stifling Congress, and—of course—assassination. Surely his 1962 "Man on the Moon" speech became magical, as countless others and I watched—in black and white—the Apollo 11 landing on the moon in the summer of 1969. The highlight reel of the decade included Martin Luther King's famous

"I Have a Dream" speech, the Vietnam war and the passing of the Civil Rights Act. On the lighter side, we witnessed the British Invasion, the first *Bond* Movie, and, of course, "Here's ... Johnny". And, on the *higher* side: Woodstock in 1969.

The decade, in general, was described as one of a revolution in social reform, while conservatives described the tenure as a decay of moral fiber. Remember: this was the hippie love-and-peace decade. While there were dark moments, apparently some people thought others were having too much fun.

How did I view the '60's? Frankly, they were magical childhood years. Winthrop Road was a mecca of sporting and other activities. My weekly piano lessons were in constant conflict with curb ball, stickball, football, hockey, basketball, ice skating, fort building, fishing, snake hunting, bicycle explorations, stealing and running the bases, stealing Johnny's shoes, igloo building, tree climbing, swimming, crayfish hunting, salamander hunting, scouting and camping. The list goes on. Piano never had a chance. It seemed I was stuck on Beethoven's "Fur Elise" for years, despite the rewards of model airplanes and race cars.

Oh, my goodness, how could I forget the pets? You name it, we had it—and mother had had it many times as well (up to her neck). There were chickens, tropical fish, salt-water fish, gerbils, hamsters, ferrets, tadpoles, frogs, snakes, lizards, turtles, cats and mating *Hyalophora cecropia* moths. The highlight reel was topped when my mother walked into a garage of twenty-five escaped new-born garter snakes, but surely the birthing of baby gerbils on New Year's Eve and the fluorescing of leaping frogs' stomachs—as they snatched trapped fireflies—were wonderful as well.

From sun up to sun down, we all were about. A favorite getaway was a tract of land and lake once dedicated to a communication station the US Navy took over in 1917 to provide wireless communications overseas during WW I. Eventually taken over by the company RCA, the concrete bunkers for towers were clearly visible as friends and I made our way to RCA lake, where countless hours were spent *not* catching fish. It was surely worth the six-mile bike trip, made as early as dawn some summer mornings.

In the evening, after these exhausting days, I would lay on my grandmother's bed. Irma and I would watch the New York Yankees and the Honeymooners, enjoying Jackie Gleason's daily sending of Alice to the moon, and Art Carney's limber-limb theatrics, as he and Jackie engaged in senseless banter.

They are, indeed, fond memories—certainly devoid of responsibility, and oblivious to the harshness of world events, but I believe a source of happiness and joy all wish to find and live by. I did find it again, but would lose it for quite some time—a very long time. A single insignificant event at the age of fifteen would suffice to trigger an unimaginably painful illness. I'll tell you how.

Open your heart son, and let your emotions paint the pages with words of passion!

CHAPTER 5

A TROT BACK IN TIME

I will admit during the 1970s, I watched Tattoo announce, "De plane, de plane, de plane!" to introduce each Fantasy Island episode. And yes, I enjoyed the honking of Horshak and the confusion of Vinnie Barbarino on Welcome Back, Kotter. But will I admit I enjoyed the theme song to Love Boat every week? Absolutely not. Nor will I admit I pranced around in platform shoes and wore some pretty-psychedelic-polyester prints from the waist up, and some flaring bells from the waist down. Did I use a hairdryer, meticulously grooming my golden lengthy locks before the ride to school—no, no, no, no, no!

I will admit, us neighborhood guys were pretty cool, chilling out in our white Chuck Taylor Converse Sneakers. Even cooler, we just said, "Cons man. Just plain 'Cons." Clyde and the Knicks, the Ali vs. Frazier fights, "Sweet Lou" and Thurman also defined a certain coolness, class, athletic grit and professionalism for the decade.

But, while integrity and heart were being displayed on the hard court and in the ring, there were some difficulties in D.C., resulting in our 37th President of the United States having to resign. On the much brighter side, the Vietnam Conflict ended, and resolve to end the conflicts of its origin—and purpose—could begin.

On the science side, Steven Hawking's discovery of black holes made us humans a bit more aware. It led to an explosion of knowledge that surely should make us human beings live with a bit more humility, and leave us a bit more pliable in thought and possibility. After all, today the work of the Kepler planet-spotting spacecraft has already revealed over 3,000 life-candidate planets, and the notion there are billions in the Universe is statistically real. Maybe we don't have all the answers, after all?

And finally, of course, the music of the '70s into the '80s was pretty magical; and I might add played daily—and often—into the twenty-first century. The "Boss" and Clarence were rocking at the Jersey Shore, while lighter progressive rock bands like Kansas, Journey, Boston, Foreigner, Chicago and Styx were gaining acclaim elsewhere. Disco and the Bee Gees left millions dancing at discothèques and punk rock had listeners underground, but only Springsteen had them dancing in the streets. It was simply a wonderful era of bands and energy: artistry at every level—vocals; meaningful, often heartbreaking lyrics; dancing instruments and stage and performance energy live—just simply pure energy.

I entered my teenage years enjoying life—full of energy, drive and ambition. I was excelling in academics, music and athletics. I enjoyed friendships. No longer was I simply waking the boys up at the crack of dawn to play stick ball; this hormonally-charged adolescent was corralled toward a new species: called the female.

My body had entered puberty. The physiological changes during puberty can be rapid, and those changes may not always occur smoothly. I myself may have had such a "hiccup". As we all know, graduation into puberty allows us humans to reach sexual maturity, so reproduction becomes possible. I'd like to further define some events at puberty you might not be familiar with, so this journey into the mind-body-life connection can become complete in the end.

There is nothing wrong, but everything right with hope!

CHAPTER 6

PARENTS: READ AND BEWARE

It has long been known the teenager of the human species can quite frankly be a pain in the buttocks for the surrounding population, older and younger. I am, by no means, comparing the emerging adolescent's environmental clashes with those of the overpowering hormonal imbalances of the Vulcan-male Spock's experience into pon farr, where insanity—even death—might follow. But the term raging hormones has been a popular descriptor for us beings during this time. We experience mood instabilities and exhibit adverbs such as annoying, reckless, defiant and impulsive. We may very well have created the P.I.T.A. acronym. The word obnoxious might best sum this period of 'growth' for some, not all. No need to ruin sales.

Jesting aside, the good news is recent scientific evidence sheds much light on what is occurring physiologically during this time. The developmental changes of the brain, and the rest of the body, are both large and rapid during this time. Let's take a much-needed overview of how these changes evolve during puberty.

Let's first examine how complex the human brain is. Consider that just one cubic millimeter of human brain matter has between thirty-five and seventy million neurons, and an estimated 500 billion synapses. Modern man's brain volume reaches 1,330,000 cubic millimeters. The total amount of neurons (between 46,550,000,000,000 and 93,100,000,000,000) and synapses (66,500,000,000,000,000) is staggering. Let's see if the publisher checks these numbers – good luck.

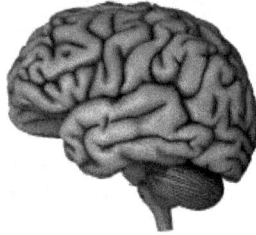

Let's make this thing a bit more complex. The above CEO/Captain, Mr. Brain, is running a ship that has over ninety trillion cells—quite a few shipmates, eh? It's time to send the ship through the storm of puberty. Here's what goes on.

During early adolescence, neurons (grey matter) and synapses (spaces between neurons) proliferate and peak in the cerebral cortex. The cerebral cortex is the seat of thought and memory processing. These same neurons and synapses are gradually pruned back until the brain is finally mature, in the early 20s. The decline that occurs is thought to have value in maximizing brain efficiency and reducing impulsivity. I gather many parents of teens would see value in an 'impulsivity reduction'. With that said, I'm sure they would like the whole *pon farr* redesigned—or eliminated!

While Mom and Dad are thinking logically, eventually more than 40% of synapses have been eliminated, largely in the frontal lobes during the process. The myelin-insulating coat on the axons of nerve cells continues to expand and accumulate. More insulation (white matter) translates to improved precision and efficiency of neuronal communication. The connection between the right and left hemisphere, or corpus callosum, consists of mostly white matter—so again, advanced communication.

The boat rocks a bit more at adolescence with another area of maturation in the circuit, linking the prefrontal cortex to the midbrain reward system. The midbrain reward system is where addictive drugs and romantic love seem to exert much influence. The adolescent brain has been known to be hypersensitive to novel experiences, and most addictions begin in adolescence. Vulnerability to peer pressure is highest at this time as well.

Some of the last changes in the maturation process involve the connections between the prefrontal cortex (judgment and problem-solving) and the emotional centers in the limbic system, especially the amygdala. Such connections are essential for emotional learning and high-level self-regulation.

While brain neurons, synapses and myelin are riding these powerful winds, the boat is being tossed by turbulent hormonal waters. The teen brain begins to pour out adrenal stress hormones, sex hormones and growth hormones, which—in themselves—affect brain structural development. Guys, the testosterone wave increases tenfold during puberty; gals, we're sorry!

These sex hormones affect the limbic system and the raphe nucleus, the source of production for the neurotransmitter serotonin. This key biochemical is a major player in the regulation of arousal and mood, and is possibly one key player in my own turbulent story. In closing, but by no means complete, these hormones reset the twenty-four-hour clock of the suprachiasmatic nucleus in the adolescent, making very cranky home-room students and very late night *Tonight Show* viewers. This nucleus is the part of the brain controlling circadian rhythms.

The labyrinth and complex processes at work at puberty undoubtedly and statistically increase the chances for mistakes. Some of these mistakes include the onset of psychiatric disorders. Two such examples include a correlation between stress in puberty and a growth delay in the hippocampus; this part of the brain is vital to memory consolidation. There is also a link of grey matter pruning and/or myelin thickening to the emergence of schizophrenia in late adolescence.

I, like all of you, was sent into this complex and raging storm. I hit a big wave, capsized and submerged. I would eventually emerge though: rescued by many of you, and finally rescued by myself—thirty-one years later! Let me tell you how. Let me tell you how it began.

Open your heart son, and let your emotions paint the pages with words of passion!

CHAPTER 7

EMERGING STORM

My first year in high school was coming to an end. Academics proceeded without a hitch, weekly Tuesday night Boy Scout meetings brought comradery and new adventures, and I had the privilege of playing baseball with a great group of guys and coach. We enjoyed a successful frosh-spring baseball season.

An annual routine eye exam with my ophthalmologist during the last days of my freshman year would serve to trigger a most crippling painful disorder, and disrupt my life for the next thirty-one years.

As my mother Claire sat in the waiting room, Dr. Bloom proceeded with his examination. The standard switching of lenses and reading of black A Q Z U V's, while alternating between left and right eyes, was relatively uneventful. I did notice some blurring on the periphery of letters. They were not quite as sharp as in previous years, but we were done.

Dr. Bloom jotted down some notes and nonchalantly concluded, "Rob, your eyes are no longer 20/20; you're a bit nearsighted, but they'll be no need for a prescription."

"A prescription for what?" I asked.

"Well, glasses," he replied.

It simply pains me to write, this is all that happened. It is simply incomprehensible how such a simple event would cascade uncontrollably to other events, and change things for thirty-one years until 2009, when I finally asked, "What if?"

Let me tell you how the bizarre would lead to the even more bizarre, so you might understand the very nature, biochemistry and physiology of obsessive-compulsive disorder, and the mechanisms of medications taken.

There is nothing wrong, but everything right with hope!

CHAPTER 8

ORIGIN OF A NIGHTMARE

The effect of the ophthalmologist's exam was immediate. My thoughts were alarming to me, because I immediately could sense they were not going to stop. Not only was I worried and fearful of something within this eye examination, but there was an added layer of fear: the stressful, burdensome state of mind I was experiencing was not going away anytime soon. Fear atop fear, double trouble indeed. My mind had gone rogue.

And so, as my mother and I began our drive home, let me drive you—the reader—into the very components of a thought process gone awry that would riddle me with pain and exhaustion, and drive me to levels of unimaginable, wearing stress. These thoughts and state of mind would later be defined with the diagnostic term of OCD. I choose more succinct terms: hot, melting pain, unrelenting stress and exhausting anxiety.

As we headed east down Easton Avenue, I began to study the license plate on the vehicle in front of us. "Mom, can you read that license plate for me?" She read the alphanumeric combination aloud. She saw what I saw. I felt a moment of comfort. Perhaps five seconds worth.

"Mom, does the second letter look a bit blurry around the edges?"

"No, it is very clear."

My eyes saw a slight blurring around the edges. My discomfort began again.

And so, the questions and answers on visual acuity continued on the trip home. I asked about letters on signs, number of people in far-off tennis courts, and if she could see the acorn in the squirrel's mouth atop the Sycamore tree as we pulled in front of 16 Winthrop Road.

The desire for assurance outpaced the embarrassment of each question I asked. It was as if I was, in some bizarre manner, attempting to undo what the doctor had told me. I was so invested in this loop of thought I never even attempted to analyze it, or to even confront my concern. I simply felt stress. I felt hot. I felt mental pain and torture, and a physical drain. I felt I was unable to stop the thoughts or the checks. I was in an obsessive thought pattern, unable to dissect it for understanding, nor stop or control it. The latter, lost control of reasoning, was most concerning of all. It generated major levels of fear.

"Rob, are you OK?" Mom asked.

The one-tenth of my brain still in the present responded with a deceptive chuckle, "Sure, just checking."

The other nine-tenths of my brain, invested in the absurd, was in dread. *What was going on? Why was I short-circuiting in the early summer of 1978? Why did the endless loop happen again—and again and again? I was no longer the captain of the ship!*

I knew I was no longer in control of my brain, and that very knowledge petrified me—although at the time I did not recognize it. I was fearful, and the fear of lost control drove the loop around and round. Being totally absorbed in the absurd left me unable to even contemplate a solution.

I'll never forget that hour after the eye exam, but I certainly wish I could. I say this because the brain-lock I was in, one of mental pain, anguish and stress, would last another three years and seven months; yes, another 31,000 hours. The horrific obsessions even plagued my sleep.

I did receive one small break though. It was a magical month or so, at one of North Carolina's major universities in the spring of 1981. I will tell you about my time in North Carolina, but even more importantly, how I used this bizarre halt in my obsessional lock as a key piece of evidence to find a cure for myself.

In 2009, I would take a retrospective analysis of my illness, and my time in North Carolina was one of the key events that led to me finding a cure for my OCD—including any and all side effects and sequelae resulting from the medications taken for OCD.

I'll tell you about college life, the cure, love, family and so much more in the pages to come.

Open your heart, and let your emotions paint the pages with words of passion, inspiration and knowledge!

CHAPTER 9

REBIRTH

To my reader, I must apologize. To the over 2% estimated worldwide individuals suffering from OCD, and the 25% afflicted with mental illness at some point in their life, I—in good conscience—had to pick up the pen again. Almost three years after writing Chapter 8, I have resumed the hope my words will flow unrestricted.

The wonderful news is I have now been symptom-free for over nine years. It further validates my theories I am convinced have worldwide applications—not only for OCD—but for misdiagnosed bipolar and depression patients. They may possibly help those suffering from anorexia nervosa, bulimia and body-dysmorphic syndrome. The latter three illnesses are known to share overlap with OCD symptomatology. I will explain later, as the story of my analysis of the history of my thirty-one-year ordeal unfolds. It has led me to view the overlap, and potential help for these other disorders.

The other wonderful news is I have learned much about life in these three years. Most importantly, I learned an individual who never suffered the brain-lock of OCD does not understand the severity of the disorder. This makes sense, but the lack of comprehension is further magnified by how OCD is defined, typically as "exaggerated worry" or "background thoughts", which of course we all have. I cannot tell you how painful initially it was for me to hear, "Robert, I worry too!" My jaw almost drops, but then I realized this uneducated—yet understandable—thinking, is ubiquitous.

As mentioned, medical dictionaries do mention the ritualistic activity of OCD patients and their purpose: the reduction of anxiety. In this chapter, I will offer my own definition of obsessive-compulsive disorder/neurosis to offer a bit more clarity. But first, I would like to relay why I put the pen down—and what prompted me to pick it back up again.

My words stopped flowing thirty-three months ago, out of concern the writing would affect my employment status. I have a wonderful wife, and two beautiful daughters, now five and six. Recent economic turmoil in this great land of ours led me to this very sad decision. Two recent events have propelled me forward. I am also going to place a bit more trust in the minds of my fellow man, and their views of my words. Lastly, in good conscience, I cannot keep quiet—I want no one to suffer as I did, and others have and do. Let me explain what reinvigorated me.

As I awaited and prepared for a business meeting about one year ago at a local coffee shop, the table abutting my dwarfish "desk-table" was filled by two women. The two inches separating our life environments offered little privacy, and I could not help but notice tears and anguish flowing from one of the women, the other consoling her as best she could.

I continued an attempt at reviewing several orthopedic solutions for a materials manager at a local hospital, but the conversation between these two hurting souls became impossible to ignore. The woman to my left, tearful, face covered in hair—spoke of an ordeal. Her now seventeen-year-old daughter was suffering horribly from OCD. The ordeal had already torn apart her marriage. The daughter, like me, was very successful in high school, but her existence—well, both existences—were in shambles. As the conversation ensued, it seemed the mom was at an absolute loss to understand the syndrome, and might possibly be underestimating the severity of it. Nonetheless, and as mentioned above, she was amongst many who do not understand the pain and stress the OCD patient feels.

After ten minutes of this conversation, I could no longer keep quiet. I no longer cared. I wanted to help these two people. I told my story and offered hope and phone numbers. Oddly enough, the mother's friend was the more overjoyed of the two. She was more open and excited about my ideas. I was offering hope and a possible solution for this young seventeen-year old. The mother seemed skeptical and—in retrospect—I guess maybe I would be, too. Both were extremely grateful for my help though.

I asked the mother to have the girl call me; I was someone who understood. While speaking with the mother, she asked a question that led me to understand another misconception about my illness. She doubted my words. *How could I be cured? How could I be totally cured?*

Well, here's the thing I told her. The obsessive thoughts were nonstop for me. When one set of thoughts ended, they only ended because another set took their place. So, if I am cured of OCD and have control of my thoughts, and no longer have obsessions, they are totally gone.

At least for me, they are either totally unrelenting and nonstop, or they don't exist at all—which has been true for last eight years.

The mother asked me, "How do you know it will never come back?"

I went on to explain the last seven years had been very stressful for my family and me. So, even under extreme duress, my symptoms had not returned. I did confide in the woman the following, which did elicit a smile from her friend:

I explained if the things I do to keep myself healthy are taken from me; if Earth is hit with a meteor, evaporating mankind; my only remaining companionship and meal plan include malaria-laden mosquitos and subway super rats—then yes, perhaps I might have a return in symptoms.

I never heard back from the mother, and I did check with the physician I referred her to. Of course, patient-client permission may be an explanation. I hope mom, daughter and friend read my book.

Then in 2017, I had a meeting with a prominent New Jersey professional. A thirty-five-minute meeting, and I could not thank the gentleman more. My face glowed when he read my theories and said, "Robert, finish your book."

He said, "Don't worry about the biochemistry and anatomy and medical details—you can write another book with those details."

We both understood I have a background in physiology and medicine, and not everyone does. *Write the book for everyone,* we both concluded. A simple, inspiring, intriguing read was the hope for the masses. He did not charge me for the meeting (I felt his empathy, warmth and excitement), but rather asked for a copy of the book on completion. He wanted me to get the message out—and get it out fast, and so I hope to do so. Understand, this gentleman also—upon the start of the conversation—shared the same misconceptions about OCD others have. He allowed me to explain what it was like, and so I will do so below.

Please, while you read this, understand the absolute bizarreness of the state of being of an obsessive compulsive. I am going to describe to you what is occurring in my brain, a loss of control of rational thought. Yet I, like other OCD patients, live and make rational decisions and thoughts at the same time. Also, try to imagine the absolute mental pain, stress and anxiety of the OCD patient. Try to place yourself in my body and brain at age eighteen, on this day, in the winter of 1980.

I am sitting on the front steps of my home, during my senior year in high school. It is December of 1980. It is Christmas time, and my parents have friends over for a holiday party. I can hear the joy and jubilation of the holidays inside the house, but rather than being infectious, it saddens and disheartens me because of my state of health. It was a mental state unbeknownst to all except my parents. As I write, that night becomes horribly alive and vivid. Come inside my brain and body in 1980 for just a few paragraphs, please.

For the last three days, I have been obsessing about hitting someone on a local road on a Tuesday afternoon. I know the person I think I may have hit was only a wooden fence post some fifteen feet off the road, yet I keep trying to settle the dilemma. I went back to the spot several times and, with each inspection, reached the same conclusion. I did not hit anything. Each visit—defined as a ritual—offers twenty seconds of anxiety relief, but the obsession rolls back in, as do the checks or rituals. An endless cycle until an obsession of more "power" rolls in.

Still in 1980, the brisk air hits my face, and I notice a poinsettia—three feet to my left—as I sit on the front steps of 16 Winthrop Road. The party noise rolls on. I feel guilty I am not socializing with the very people who praised my scholastic and academic achievements. They want to know about college and where I will play baseball, among other things. Meanwhile, college applications swirl in my head; *Should I write about the fence post I hit in my college essay?*

As I sit, I remember the poinsettia's leaves are actually poisonous. Suddenly, I feel I have poisoned one of the party guests with one of the leaves—a plant that has not come near me. I remind myself, without effect, I haven't touched the plant, ground up the leaves or placed anything in a drink. I remind myself I have not been inside for fifteen minutes, yet I am guilty of attempted murder. The fence-post crime has disappeared. I now have sweat pouring from my forehead, as I sit in thirty-degree weather. My heart races, palms sweaty, with anxiety peaking. The Datsun B210, my car, awaits me—parked thirty feet away; I need to turn myself in to the Township Police Department. I need to go to the police station. *Good God, they'll think I am nuts.* I imagine the chat, "Officer, Robert Lindemann here to turn myself in for attempted murder."

"Hey, Rob, how does baseball season look this spring?"

"No, I am here for attempted poinsettia poisoning!"

"Okay, well—hey, Rob, uh, who did you try to kill?"

"I have no idea!"

"Ooooookay."

Now, what this confession would attempt to solve is a slight twenty-second reduction in anxiety. This visit to the police station would be medically termed as a ritual. It is a human being's attempt to solve this endless loop of brain-lock. I know it will not work to cease the thoughts, but it is all this human had left. I no longer longed *for my two front teeth* at Christmas time, I simply wanted my "marbles" back!

It is the most painful, anxiety-ridden and stressful state imaginable. To top it off, it does not exist. The dilemma does not exist. *How do you solve a loop that has no problem?*

This is how I existed for close to four years. I want no one else to have this happen to them.

With the above example noted, I would like to help expand on the definitions of OCD I have presented thus far.

<u>Obsessive-Compulsive Disorder, Redefined</u>

OCD is a disorder defined as a state of being, whereby a patient suffers from brain-lock: an endless loop of thought. It is a loop where the patient suffers mental pain, anxiety and stress, and attempts to solve the dilemma most often with fictional rituals—a series of checks that very briefly offers relief. The patient realizes the thoughts are ludicrous, yet cannot control or stop the thought process. The very notion of this loss of control evokes fear, which further perpetuates the disorder. The state of being is mentally and physically draining, and unrelenting and constant. An obsession only resolves after replacing it, at least in my experience. The patient, meanwhile, can resume what appears to be a normal life—but cannot fully invest the self to life. Most of their attention is trapped in this loop.

The state of mind also invades a patient's sleep. Understand, the ritual is but a byproduct of the main problem: lost control of thought. The disorder has a biochemical disorder component to it. In *The Lindemann Theory*, I postulate OCD thought-induced non-stop stress creates cortisol, detrimental to neurons in the hippocampus and possibly elsewhere, which helps maintain the brain-lock.

Most importantly, understand that despite the absurdity of the obsessional thoughts, they are extremely real, stress-invoking and deleterious for the patient, thereby inducing cortisol in response to long-term stress. This component is vital for the clinician to understand, and one of the main components of my theory.

While I have offered several examples of individuals correlating OCD with typical worry, perhaps on an exaggerated scale, there is one individual who confided in me an experience of brain-lock. I reached out to a local clergy one day for advice on a business matter. In this conversation, I explained my thirty-one-year ordeal, and he in turn confided in me.

He explained a period of his life, before he found his life's work, where he was lost in drug abuse. He had inhaled gasoline one night, and explained a two-minute nightmarish period where he was stuck in the type of brain-lock I described. The two minutes was described as an eternity, an endless cycle in which people rolled along a wheel, and in turn kept repeating, "Every, if, and, or, but; every, if, and or, but …" over and over again—the phrase went—and it drove this person mad.

I will assume, of course, this was a bad reaction, and not the intended one. In any event, it is medically known (not well-known), there are a few substances that can induce the brain-lock of OCD. I felt comfort in knowing this man of the cloth shook his body at the thought of a near four year ordeal in the type of brain-lock I described to him.

With Chapter 9 written, I sat in bed as my wife proofread and critiqued the material. I then walked into my sleeping six-year-old's room, and kissed my daughter, Rhaena, on the forehead. The warmth of her brow comforted me. I proceeded to my five-year-old Rochelle's room, and lay beside her with my head on her shoulder.

She whispered to me, "Now I lay me down to sleep, I pray the Lord my soul to keep. Guide me through the starry night, and wake me with the morning light. God bless Mommy and Daddy, Rhaena and Rochelle, Roger (Guinea Pig), all the fishes in the world and Jesus Christ our Lord. Amen."

There is nothing wrong, but everything right with hope!

CHAPTER 10

RAINBOW AND THE HAMMER

During the spring and summer of 1981, there was magical period of time when my OCD miraculously disappeared. This time also served as a key piece of evidence I utilized to conjure components of my theories and ultimate cure in 2009. That cure has extended well into 2017: a period of time that confirms my theory. At the time of the 1981 OCD disappearance, I did not even consider the relevance of the vanishing of those obsessions, lasting about six weeks. Other than those six weeks, there would be close to four-year, continuous battle with obsessional neurosis.

In this chapter, I will examine the rainbow that blossomed in my brain as I entered the campus of one of North Carolina's finest universities in August of 1981. The subsequent hammering storm that shattered my psyche and seared my heart will be painfully explored as well.

Let me first preface this discussion with a flashback to bits from my senior year at high school and ultimate acceptance to this fine institution in North Carolina. It was on this beautiful campus, enveloped with wonderful faculty, where I would pursue baseball on a field of dreams, academia and lifetime friendships. Already inundated with the condition of OCD for two years, going on three, my senior year's state of mind and overall health was again one of unimaginable stress, mental pain, anxiety, fog and exhaustion—above and below the neck.

This description of my senior year is quite contrary, I'm certain, to what others might have perceived. I was fortunate to have been very successful both athletically and academically, and blessed to have the local newspapers, teachers and coaches show their appreciation. My fifth-grade teacher actually mailed me a letter, describing her pride when seeing newspaper article after article, and wished me all the best as I made my way into the world.

Mrs. Novache, I still have that letter to this day. As I type, my eyes tear with joy at the beauty of your soul and spirit. Bless every teacher and coach in the Franklin Township School System—and worldwide.

Dear Robert,

I was delighted and excited to read about your wonderful achieve-ments in my local paper … copies of the clippings … I have been follow-ing your exploits … Congratulations and continued success in college...

A major Ivy League school was also impressed with what I had achieved: fifth in-class rank out of 399 students, Athlete of the Year, MVP Varsity Baseball three straight years, co-captain of a baseball team for two straight years, MVP Football Line, and Eagle Scout rec-ognition. The Ivy League school granted me the Bausch and Lomb Science Award—an academic scholarship—and I was thankful for my visit to their campus during the winter crossing 1980 and 1981. But, truth be told, folks: a walk over a suspension bridge at the school's campus, with a magnificent gorge—hundreds of feet below—hearing a chat about student suicide by my guide, did not exactly bode well for my fragile, stressed-out psyche.

I'll never forget the accolades at our high school awards dinner or having to tell a reporter post I was uninterested in a feature-article sit-down interview for the local paper. I couldn't explain how seeing my picture in the paper again, knowing how unhappy and desperate I was on the inside, would make me feel. I was barely able to wake up in the morning and embrace life. I remember the reporter's name; he was a fellow classmate, and I hope he will read this one day. Mack, I am so sorry, but I was so very sick. I hurt so bad inside with pain I want no else to feel.

That same year, my grandmother Irma—my mother's mom—died of a massive heart attack in the room next to mine. She had lived with us my whole life. Irma sensed something was wrong with me, starting in 1978. I recall, one day, her crying to my mother, "What's wrong with Robert?"

I had become distant with my grandmother once this nightmare began, and she knew I was not myself. I spent months after Irma's massive attack and death, obsessing I had flicked some pills through bedroom walls the night of the incident, and her death was my responsibility.

The family minister even got involved during this period, and he had no idea what to make of my attempt to relay what was happening to me. Thank heavens I was raised Presbyterian, not Catholic, because demonic possession would be as good a diagnosis as any I received. Although it was 1981, most of America still had the movie *The Exorcist* in their heads from 1973. After all, it is not every day one sees a human being's head spinning like a top—kind of drops your jaw and drawers, and raises one's privates.

If you thought refusing a reporter's interview at age eighteen was confusing, how about my decision to run for class president? I won—

and then the panic ensued. Here's a thought: *You are already at wits' end, why not take on more responsibility?* I went to the senior class advisor, also my Shakespeare teacher, and resigned.

It broke my heart when a fellow classmate stopped me in the hall to ask if I had done it as a publicity stunt. I had just taken a drink of water from the hall fountain when she asked, and just sprayed it out all over the floor, post her inquiry. I only wished I could tell someone about the disorder and the anguish.

The senior prom became an early evening and normal-day after-prom activities suspended, as I played in the state of New Jersey's baseball all-star game. There, I found my path to the North Carolina University, where I might place my heel in tar—and play for a fine young coach and man.

In August of 1981, my father Robert E. Lindemann and I packed the family wagon and headed to 78 West. We spent the bulk of the trip going down 81 South, and entered the wonderful university campus some ten-plus hours later. I was beautifully situated in a dorm down the right-field line of the baseball stadium and became smitten with the environment; excitement rushed through my veins and pride swelled my sternum. I fell in love with the paths of brick, amid pine-laden grounds, and the warmth and soul in those southern accents.

As I walked onto the baseball field, I felt the obsessions dissipate—then they were gone.

If memory serves me well, I arrived a couple of weeks pre-class registration, and we already were on the diamond practicing, and in the weight room pumping iron. I'll always remember that field had the thickest, plushest set of grass I've ever set foot on. I was told it was seeded with the same grass seed used at Yankee stadium. The players explained to me: this year we would not see the New York

Yankees stop over for a practice game en route to Florida, as they had in seasons past—since George Steinbrenner's daughter had graduated the previous year. I remember some of the players commenting: Mr. Gossage was not *that* fast. I chuckled at the sight of a warm-up fastball by the *Goose*, a foot above all as a reminder that: "Oh yeah!"

My coach was a young, energetic coach, who valued running and weight training, along with the basics of baseball. I'll always remember the picnic held at his house, where the players were served delicious barbecue and hush puppies. The coach placed his baby in my arms, and I felt like I was part of a family. That tiny guy would eventually become a professional baseball player, and certainly Coach had a large part in that—pride for you both.

My dorm roommate was a North Carolina resident, an apparent valedictorian of his high school, who helped train the football team. He was a great guy who started to change his voice to reflect my northern drawl—he felt his accent made him sound dumb. I told him to keep that accent, as I found the people of the South warm, charming and happy. I wish I remembered his name. I believe he wanted to become a doctor.

The baseball players, post-practice one day, spoke of going to a party that evening. They were excited about meeting a new basketball player freshman "Phenom". I was not yet familiar with the legacy of the basketball program at this school. I found their excitement to be odd, but I guess their insight was a bit more astute than mine. The kid's name carried the initials M.J. Seems he turned into a pretty good player.

Now, the training table (cafeteria) for athletes offered a whole new world to me. Situated back behind center field of the baseball stadium, I'll always remember the filled plate I had when this young student came over, sat down and introduced himself to me. The gentleman was a golfer, one of a famous golfer's sons: most likely the greatest of golfers. As we spoke, the corner of my eye realized I had a plate filled with massive quantities of mashed potatoes and a lake of gravy—on the scale of the Great Lakes combined. That training table was a dangerous place to be.

I met a very nice, young southern belle during class registration. Academics, baseball and my social life were underway. I was extremely happy, and having fun on the baseball diamond. While my bat was alive and hammering, my arm struggled from an injury towards the end of my high school season while pitching. My shortstop play was hindered, due to a two-year leave from the position, as I pitched most of my junior and senior year. But again, I was thrilled to be at this institution.

The coach approached me one day and asked, "Why in the world were you driving along a major roadway at about fifty miles per hour, downhill, on your bike?"

I laughed it off, but avoided mentioning the half-hour weekly trip to the psychologist I was set up with upon entrance to the school. The psychologist could not understand the absolute absence of symptoms, and I never questioned the return of joy to my life. I was fifteen years old again—and the pain of the last three years was over. I just rejoiced. I was alive. I was free!

I rolled into September, and quizzes and tests came and went. The stress of academics, baseball and a campus environment increased just a bit. The baseball players were asked to study as a group at night, and that was unusual for me. I was also asked to tutor as well. It represented a very small conflict and bit of stress. This, along with a few very minor stressful events—I can only postulate now—were enough to bring the obsessions back at full force.

In *The Lindemann Theory*, I hypothesize a connection between stress in the creation and maintenance of the syndrome of OCD, with the understanding an adolescent biochemical storm is in place. I then later explore methods of cortisol reduction, utilizing *InfinitE/ IQ*.

I was beyond devastated when the obsessions returned in full force. Not only had the mental pain returned, but my heart and drive were absolutely shredded. I was now alone, ten hours from home, and in agony. I recall a tactic in warfare, where the troops are lulled into thinking they had become victorious—and then an all-out attack is initiated by the enemy with great effect. The heart of the troops is taken.

It was a devastating feeling for me to find peace and joy, and then become suffocated—unexpectedly—by pain.

I called my father in New Jersey, and he began his trip to North Carolina. I explained to the coach what was occurring, but I do not think he understood. I can't blame him. No one understood. He sat me down and said a prayer with me. I said goodbye to no one except him. I had no idea what to tell anyone. I was lost in a vacuum. Not only was the mental pain of the obsessions omniscient, but an air of depression started to seep in. I dealt with the agony for three years at high school, but when they returned the way they did—I can only say I was so very, very lost.

I loved that place, you have no idea! North Carolina was my rainbow. The hammer and the storm fell and hit, the brain-lock returned and depression began its insidious creep. I would use the rainbow at North Carolina though, to break the lock for good in 2009: just thirty-one years later—both a blip and never-ending journey in time!

I can still smell the grass, still feel my cleats upon the earth, still smell the needles of white pine and still feel my heart was molded in tar – that's just the way it is, I'm not sure it will ever change.

Open your heart, and let your emotions paint the pages with words of passion, inspiration and knowledge!

Pinus Strobus
Eastern White Pine

CHAPTER 11

RUBBER BANDS AND TRICKLING STREAMS

Before we delve back into the story, I would like to again clarify the thought patterns and behaviors behind my own OCD disorder. I want the reader to understand the content of these obsessions to be irrelevant in terms of interpretation—but to the patient the content is real and damaging. The pattern, of course, equates to a concern (perhaps a worry for the healthy mind) that becomes extraordinarily magnified to the brain-locked individual. The OCD patient seeks to resolve the issue with continued "rational" cognition, or rituals and checks, which provide seconds of relief. Knowing the failures of these checks, the individual returns to the rituals anyway.

Why? Why does one keep going back to the same unsuccessful coping mechanisms?

For me personally, and I gather others, the obsessional thoughts are so powerful and all-consuming, one loses their ability to enter creative problem-solving. The brain of the OCD patient is not quiet and relaxed, a condition needed for quality analytical thought. It is this latter thought—in itself—that concerns me. For cognitive and behavioral approaches to be successfully broken, the lock of the OCD patient must be broken. This concept is also part of *The Lindemann Theory.*

Physical health, mental health and relationships are dramatically effected by the condition. There is no resolution to the concern. Rather, the obsession only becomes immaterial on the substitution of another worry, which transcends immediately to a new obsession. The ridiculous becomes mundane, when the more ridiculous holds more power—pretty crazy stuff, right, folks!

Imagine the frustration and the fear of lost control, and of the never-ending—and always substituted—concerns. These obsessions are at the fore, while the patient's daily life activities are in the background of thought.

For purposes of accuracy, I have and will continue to relay some of the actual obsessions that took place during these times. You will notice one overriding theme: the thoughts may very well be concerns any healthy brain finds resolution to—or at least does not represent a constant intrusive, unsolvable dilemma for the human mind. The ability to dismiss separates a healthy mind from an OCD-riddled mind. The inability to dismiss frightens the OCD patient. Fear—a strong accelerator—along with long-term stress-induced cortisol production, maintains the lock. Imagine a wheel spinning in oil, the oil always inhibiting the brake system although it is there. And so, the wheel goes around and round.

My story began describing a simple eye exam turned nightmare. Despite having a class in sexual education in junior high school, I was still unprepared for the urges and completion of self-gratification, as adolescent fantasies pervaded my adolescent brain. So, within one period of masturbation, I had convinced myself I was now gay. And so, within a few weeks I had gone from going blind to being gay.

My wife, who grew up in Guyana, had a similar adolescent scare, upon her first menstruation at age fifteen. My beautiful wife, Rosanne, reasonably assumed she was dying upon blood being expelled from her body. Once explained to her, she resolved the concern and went on with life. Had my wife been in a state of brain-lock, despite the explanation, she would have continued to believe she was going to die.

To draw a comparison, I had sexual intercourse as a teen, and obsessed I had gotten the young lady pregnant. Now, even after the gal had her period, I still obsessed she was going to get pregnant—hence, the inability to resolve what is obvious to the healthy mind.

There is purpose in me repeating these points over and over to you, the reader. That point is part of my overall theory in the treatment of OCD, with perhaps overlap to the anorexics, bulimics and the body dysmorphics. These syndromes are highly resilient to traditional methods of non-pharmaceutical therapy—and for very good reason. The maintenance of the misery is physiological, I believe, and representative of altered, abnormal neurotransmitter levels— quite simple, unhealthy brain chemistry.

Can the origins of these illnesses have a psychological or environmental influence? Yes, I believe so. Can they be unlocked by psychotherapy? I believe this to be difficult, and part of my theory suggests a pharmaceutical remedy to break the lock. But with that said, the very drugs that eliminated my OCD symptoms created a myriad of unexplained new ones. I will explore all of this in detail later.

At age fifteen—riddled with OCD—my parents took me to Dr. Paulette, a clinical psychologist in the New Jersey area. Our work began. I described to Dr. Paulette my fantasy of "going down on myself" and—in turn—asked if was gay. Dr. Paulette was quick to quip, "Are you very flexible?"

Well, at least my doctor had a sense of humor.

While Dr. Paulette's diagnosis of an obsessional-neurosis disorder was accurate, his modes of therapy proved futile—and actually increased pain levels. The latter, my own quip. Dr. Paulette placed a rubber band on my right wrist and asked me to snap it every time I had an obsession. This is termed an aversion therapy. In the continuation of extreme witticism, I would more accurately describe it as amputation therapy.

Couple the therapy with my Type-A and diligent demeanor: I followed directions to the tee. And so, I snapped that rubber band nonstop, as the obsessions were nonstop. Had it not been for entrance to sleep, I honestly believe I would have snapped my right wrist off.

Certainly, this may have resolved the masturbation issue, unless I added ambidexterity to increased spinal hyperflexion. One week later, I returned to Dr. Paulette. He, indeed, showed concern over the painful, red laceration revolving around my wrist. I now understand—understandably so—Dr. Paulette and most of my physicians had no concept of what was occurring in my brain. What an advantage it would be to have a doctor who actually first-hand experienced the distress of such psychiatric disorders.

Next, Dr. Paulette gave me a series of cassettes with natural sounds, such as waterfalls. We embarked on relaxation therapy. Again, this had no effect. In addition to pain, I now felt the frustration of knowing that not only me and others—but the medical community itself—found this illness mysterious and "untreatable". The most twisted part of the illness is the anxiety that exists in the OCD patient, being generated by the OCD thoughts themselves.

You may recall the coffee-shop chat I had with the mother of the OCD daughter. The daughter was being given anti-anxiety medication atop her OCD medications, which—in my opinion—is useless and complicates the efficacy of the OCD medications. Stop the thoughts, and the anxiety will disappear. Neurochemistry is complex and the result of millions of years of evolution. Do not complicate an OCD cocktail with anti-anxiety medications. Anxiety is a secondary manifestation of the primary problem: a distortion of the fine balance of brain chemistry that led to the brain-lock. The origin of the lock could be physiological, psychological or a combination of both.

Make no mistake in my comments above, folks. Talk therapy, aversion therapy, exposure therapy and all means of psychotherapy have tremendous value in many aspects of struggling human interactions and mental illnesses. But, I believe they should be presented carefully to the OCD patient, if at all. My concern here is the outrageous pain level and chances of suicidal ideation.

View the above thoughts with an open mind, and I will discuss breaking the cycle of brain-lock with pharmacologic intervention. Then, I will present my ideas for the eventual removal of such agents and why, and introduce *InfinitE/IQ*.

I found Dr. Paulette to be a warm and caring person; perhaps just as frustrated as myself. As a parent of a five and six-year old, I now understand what my parents must have been going through. They never gave up. I owe my life to them. There is a very good reason I chose my father to be my best man at my wedding. Quite frankly, he saved my life. His actions kept me alive long enough for me to put the puzzle together in 2009.

Keep reading. The roller coaster is just starting.

There is nothing wrong, but everything right with hope!

CHAPTER 12

BEST MAN, BEST DAY AND BEST BIRTH

It was a night neither of us had great enthusiasm to head out in. Friday night out with the boys and girls, post a hectic work day, was the goal. And so, in late January of 2006, we worked our way to a local lounge in northern New Jersey. While we were captivated by each other on the dance floor that night, truth be told, we were both transfixed by the dance moves of a gentleman—probably in his 80s. Double-jointed genetically—or by arthritic decay—was the debate in hand.

He basically made the action in the '87 flick *Dirty Dancing* seem prudish. His circular hand motions about his loin and mid-section gyrations left us wonderfully smiling—with 911 cell phones ready. Opening lines and awkward conversations were avoided, as the pounding base from the subwoofers forced—at least me—into lip-reading mode. It was a wonderful night. I fell in love, and while her early departure from the scene left me a bit concerned, her four-a.m. call to my apartment cemented the bond.

Rosanne is Guyanese. She was raised in British Guyana, and arrived at the shores to become a citizen of the United States at age thirteen. A beautiful story of grit and determination in her own right, and that of her mother and brothers, Rosanne is both strong and lovely at the same time. Neither of us asked each other a lot of questions about our past, and by Valentine's Day we were both smitten.

My mother's most-generous donation of three family stones, crafted into a beautifully designed engagement ring, was in my pocket as we ascended to the Top of the Rock Observation Deck in New York City's Rockefeller Center. Thankfully, my soon-to-be wife did not question the coat I was wearing, which concealed the gift—the late September weather did not warrant the attire. This was my biggest concern; my love for her leveled trepidation or hesitation.

Rosanne was wonderfully surprised. I received a resounding, "Yes!" and the folks on the deck clapped in joy. The certainty of my love for her left me without nerves, so there was no excuse when I failed to get on one knee. Post-acceptance, Rose's right hand on my shoulder forced me to my knees (a redo). All of us were able to do the proposal a second time—and with equal results. I had never proposed before, if this helps. It helped me.

I asked Rosanne about the coat I was wearing that night: "Did you not think it unusual?" I would learn later in my marriage, Rosanne comes from an equatorial territory where—on this particular type of night—a coat was warranted. Apparently, my Norwegian and German blood allows me to enjoy riding in the car in the winter with the windows open, and sleep at night with the window ajar. Apparently, the cold bite freezing one to sleep is not the norm. A hypothermic-induced caloric bleed, while in deep sleep to enjoy maximum-growth hormone release, seems an exciting option for me.

The answer is "no" to the reader, to the question, "Have Rose and I resolved this temperature dilemma?" Wool fibers and down stuffing have been used to warm the human body through the ages; the former first spin in 1900 BC. Now, think of the energy savings and added excitement in me accessing the goody baskets, if my wife adorned these garments for a harmonious milieu of temperature. Yet, after nine years of marriage … still unresolved. What would Jesus do? I dwell here—so sorry, let me move on.

To dwell is human;
Worry can be trite,
Yet a tad to push forward if one's stalled in flight,
but excessive anxiety, driven by fear—
Unharnessed it can drive one quickly to tears. RWL

I have written this poem to help humans examine the phenomenon of worry.

The human condition of worry—if understood properly—can be harnessed and actually utilized, full force. Worry, of course, is generated by fear. We are looking to harness the origin of fear. An example of fear and worry most of us are familiar with is the preparation and taking of an academic test. Let us harness fear and worry to our advantage here.

If the individual needs fear and worry to motivate them to study harder, then by all means—allow the fear to initiate study sessions. With this said, do not allow the fear to drive the sessions. Do not rush the study session and partake in a barrage of memorization tactics. Read, write, diagram, speak, discuss and combine thought to action to initiate learning. We will learn later, memory involves several brain areas, so connect the dots into, and on, all.

Once you put this into practice and test time arrives, take control of fear and understand it. The brain, under stress and in a worrisome state, does not lead to rational thought. So, whether one is prepared for a test or not, worry can only have negative consequences. Remind yourself of this and you will find the worry dismissed, and your best performance will occur. Take control of fear, and you can make it an asset—in any situation. While fear can have purpose, unexamined fear can create chaos, and—yes—pathology. *InfinitE/IQ*, which I will introduce soon, can prevent the progression. If pathology hits, *InfinitE/IQ* can be your final escape; it was for me.

Was my OCD created by fear? I am convinced my OCD was the result of a neurotransmitter-predisposition deficit that allowed a biochemical storm. I believe the chaos had some origin in worry, fear and stress. Unharnessed, it erupted with brain changes during adolescence and an unhealthy teen diet. Does this matter? Yes, because in 2009 I cured myself, so keep reading on.

Are we talking semantics? No, we are talking about understanding human psychology (part of human physiology), and understanding there are times where physiological processes are errant and unable to be corrected by psychotherapy. Alternatively, there are conditions where psychotherapy can suffice. The difference matters greatly. An improper and ineffective mental health protocol can lead to death and suicide—the statistics are staggering! Had I possessed a crystal ball—and knew I would be plunged into a state of OCD in the summer of 1978—would an understanding of the human condition of worry be preemptive to a disorder onset?

I believe this to be possible. But with that said, the elements promoting my final cure would have been necessary in compliment: the elements of *InfinitE/IQ*. Let me return to the struggles, beauty and triumphs of this life.

My engagement to Rosanne Chandra was wonderful. Then in October, just weeks later, I received a call from Rosanne's sister-in-law. Rose's vehicle had been struck by a tractor-trailer tire of a truck heading southbound on the New Jersey Turnpike, as she headed north. Rendered unconscious, her car totaled and having ricocheted off the center wall and then the side steel railings, she miraculously survived—and lay at Hackensack Medical Center. After determining she was in stable condition, I rushed towards Hackensack, the town where we first met.

When I arrived at the hospital, she was already out of the emergency room. Rosanne saw the approaching tire at the last second and was able to get her hands up: the shards of glass scarred only her hands and not her gorgeous face. She suffered a very bad concussion.

I sat next to her at bedside.

She said, "Hello," and asked, "Where's my engagement ring?"

Hospital staff had placed the ring, with other personal effects, in a safe location.

I replied, "Rose, the ring was placed in the hospital safe."

Conversation ensued in the room on how to locate the tractor trailer and the driver. Rose was silent, and about a minute passed. She then asked again, "Rob, where's my engagement ring?"

I looked at her, bewildered and concerned, and replied again, "Rose, they placed the ring in a hospital safe. The ring is fine."

This scenario took place two more times. Finally, a nurse entered the room and explained the phenomenon of remuneration, where one repeats something over and over again. She explained other symptoms of post-concussion syndrome.

The next few weeks were scary. Therapy proceeded and included remedial placement of shapes and animals together, pre-kindergarten material, and help with balance and learning to walk again. I'll never forget her first steps at her home along the sidewalk. Unable to balance, and almost toppling over, her first steps were frightening. She went from one edge of the sidewalk to the other, well beyond any description of a drunken sailor. Rose and I had an engagement party planned and were in the process of purchasing a home—actually in the final phases.

At the time, Rose was living with her parents. I moved in upon invitation, and with everyone's help, she got through it. Her brothers helped me move us into our new home. The actual move of Rose's possessions took about three hours, two of which we were in a vehicle. Hopefully she does not read this, but the engagement party was the night of the move. We were all late, and her possessions were thrown into a moving van with lightning efficacy. The actual move from the truck to our new home was twenty minutes, a pile high of shoes and clothes in the foyer of our new home. Her brothers who helped marveled at the shoes. When we sat down for the party she asked, "Did you fold everything?" and I said, "All were given high regard."

Rose's father and I went to the junkyard to reclaim possessions and to take photos. Upon seeing the vehicle, I burst into tears. I never had anything like that happen to me before, but as soon as I saw the windshield and corner braces and front of the vehicle, I was in shock—*how did she survive?* My wife did require eye surgery as she suffered slight nerve damage to one of her eyes, requiring detachment of two of her six ocular muscles. With her condition stabilized, we could begin wedding plans.

Choosing my best man was unequivocally the easiest decision I have ever had to make. Countless hours, time, money and stress-filled days were spent by my parents, searching for the best treatment option for OCD. I wrote my father a letter and told him as much. He was by my side, as were others, during the most beautiful and fun wedding. Friends and relatives danced the night away. My wife was stunning, and she glowed.

The Hawaiian Islands became our honeymoon haven. We swam with the turtles and snorkeled shipwrecks, four-wheeled plantations, explored rainforests and let the top down on the convertible as we drove along magnificent coastal highways, laden with volcanic mountains on high and gorgeous beaches down below.

We came home to a beautiful town and residence in Fanwood,

New Jersey. Greeted by wonderful neighbors, it was time to fill the bedrooms, and so Rose became pregnant with our first child. We read books, and Rosanne played Mozart atop her swelling mid-section. We watched our beautiful baby girl develop through the wonders of ultrasound photography. The chosen name was Rhaena Rose Lindemann, and her room was rolled in pigments of Chinese Jade and adorned with floating butterflies. I almost had an orgasm when I discovered residue-free duct tape to affix the mahogany-stained letters that spelled her name. And yes—I started to sprint about the commercial home centers, as my "new" 1926 home said "Fix, feed and adorn me."

Of course, the roads were laden with snow and ice, as Rose's water broke—and our fifty-minute ride to the hospital began. My recollection of the birth is as follows.

Rose was watching the preparation of French Onion Soup on the big screen; her mother crossing her heart in religious appeal/panic; the nurse sitting on Rosanne's chest, pushing on her stomach; my left hand fighting for survival as Rose gripped forcefully; the obstetrician with a strange apparatus on a crowning head and general room chaos. That is the visual.

I suppose my question to the panting, perspiring, womb-pushing mid-wife nurse was untimely? Yes, I asked how remarkable it was evolution had created such a tiny hole for such a large, crowning head? I mean, after all, my daughter was stuck at the doorway to life; I was curious.

I mean, did the midwife have to shout and propel sweat, "How would you like it if your penis had a football coming out of it?"

Well, you know what I said, "I wouldn't like it!" I was fearful of that woman, and yes, a tad hurt. To tell you the truth, the whole thing had that Linda Blair feel to it. I still can't shake that movie.

Then Rhaena Rose Lindemann emerged, and tears rolled from my eyes. As Rosanne held Rhaena she cried as well, as did Grandma Evelyn. Rhaena Rose was born, enveloped in a permanent golden tan, and a new American family had begun.

They call it the cycle of life: birth and death. Since the beginning of time, man has struggled with the questions surrounding pain, death and tragedy. I am no different—not arrogant to profess answers, but chuckle at those who do with sermonic loquaciousness. While the beautiful evening of our wedding proceeded, no one knew my father and best man had a malignant cancerous growth within his bladder the size of a baseball. A squamous cell carcinoma it was, just itching to find an external blood supply to invade the rest of my father's body. He would never see my first-born, Rhaena, or my second-born, Rochelle, but I feel his presence every day.

Dad told me to open my heart and let my emotions paint these pages for you with words of passion, inspiration and knowledge. I am trying. Remember, there is nothing wrong, but everything right with hope. He looks down from the heavens and continues to tend his flock. Heck, why not, a tearful and angry, "Amen to that, brother!"

Open your heart, and let your emotions paint the pages with words of passion, inspiration and knowledge!

CHAPTER 13

THANK HEAVEN FOR LITTLE SEIZURES AND STEM CELLS

The reverberation of my wife's brain against her skull, which so defines the concussion she received back in 2006, has reminded me of how minor insults to the brain were actually instrumental in saving my life.

I would like to thank the staff at the Belle Mead, New Jersey ECT Unit for allowing me to re-visit back in 2014, as discussed in Chapter 2. Of course, an additional huge thanks to the ECT Unit and the facility for saving my life on more than one occasion.

At the end of Chapter 3, I described a horrible evening of attempted escape, both from the halls of the hospital—and from my time on this Earth. Driven up a tree, only to be saved by a deprivation of tree limbs, my return to the facility was met with tears, collapse and sedation.

The following morning, still hungover from the agent administered to me the prior night, and still in a dangerous depressed state, I remember the walk over to the ECT unit. I was hopeful a series of ECT, over several days or weeks, might relieve the agony within me. I could skip the normal formalities of the administration room associated with outpatients, where I would typically be greeted by Jenny, a very warm and wonderful individual. And then, post the administration room, a short meeting with a psychiatrist, to evaluate my progress.

As an inpatient, I sat in the "pre-pre-op" room, where shoes and metal valuables were removed and placed in a brown bag with my name written upon it. Procedure then required the emptying of my bladder. The next room was a staging area, where I lay on a hospital bed, draped in warm sheeting, awaiting the placement of an I.V. The nurses were very warm and reassuring, I was never anxious. I believe my own lack of anxiety was created by the very hope and necessity of the procedure. Certainly, the warmth of the staff and my confidence in the procedure, were my allies. At that point, I even had nurses share some of their own personal problems with me, knowing—I'm sure—the understanding, empathy and confidentiality of the receiving ears.

With my confidence in the procedure stated, I will note now—and elaborate later on—an extremely difficult and dangerous reaction I had to the ECT procedure years earlier. While I remember bits and pieces of the event, the reaction very much frightened the staff, as my very well-being and life were in danger. Apparently, an area of my brain they did not intend to target was over-stimulated. ECT saves lives, and in my opinion, the benefits far outweigh the concerns; I believe quantitative research confirms my impression. In 2012, almost 4,500 ECT procedures were performed at this New Jersey mental-health facility, for a perspective on the therapy's usage.

With the I.V. inserted and securely taped, I awaited a procedure in the next room. When I got the call, I was wheeled to one of several bays. The cast of characters included a nurse, anesthesiologist and a psychiatrist trained in administering the electricity to my brain; the goal is to create a small seizure. My pulse, blood pressure and E.C.G. monitoring devices were put into place.

A good therapeutic seizure lasts from thirty to ninety seconds. Medical news out of John Hopkins in 2013 describes the action of ECT on a brain protein, which leads to stem-cell stimulation. I restrain myself from elaborating more, and will reserve it for my technical writing project. Because the procedure creates heavy oral secretions, a drying agent must first be administered via I.V.

Then I awaited my favorite anesthesiologist, a very petite older woman of Chinese descent. She would approach me, carrying a very large syringe containing the anesthesia: the dose adjusted for my weight, so I'd sleep for ten minutes. She also administered a short-acting relaxant.

This wonderful woman would approach me and rub her hand atop my head in a circular motion, and then sing a well-known lullaby. Unlike other doctors, she would not let me know when she injected the anesthesia, so I would keep watch. I sing these gentle words now to my two daughters, as we swing away on area playgrounds. Tell no one, but when troubled with going to sleep, I will ring her voice in my thoughts:

You are my sunshine,
My only sunshine,
 You make me happy, when skies are gray,
You'll never know, dear,
How much I love you,
Please don't take my sunshine away.

I loved to count the seconds it took for my circulation to carry the agent to my heart, and then propel it forward on high into my brain. I knew the anesthesia had reached my brain when I became aware of the odor of the anesthesia in the olfactory bulb within my brain. I would take a quick mental visual as the drug traveled from the I.V. in my median cephalic vein up to my right ventricle, through to my left ventricle, shoot through the aorta into the common carotids, and the internal carotids and vertebral arteries forming my brain's Circle of Willis. The odor from the bulb's receptors was distinct and quite comforting.

Yes, with the receptors in the olfactory bulb of my brain being stimulated, I could literally smell the anesthesia. I can only imagine, and equate it analogously to one being blindfolded, and yet still being able to see. It was simply an odd, unique and insightful experience. By no means am I advocating this olfactory substitute to replace the steam, smell and taste emerging from my favorite dish of veal parmigiana, sided with garlic and olive-oiled spinach and shrimp.

Upon smelling the anesthesia, I would often say "Goodbye, everybody," as I awaited the unconscious state which typically proceeded a few seconds later. Just before the final eclipse, I would remember one of my favorite spectacles: the setting of the sun as my family sits at the end of a dock, legs submerged on Lake Wallenpaupack in Pennsylvania's Pike County. One minute the bulbous orange glow is there, the next second it is gone. A wonderful re-emergence of Earth's comforter the next morning is everyone's hope. In the case of ECT's anesthesia, an uneventful return to consciousness after ten minutes is the goal.

As a side note, since exposed to this odor, if ever I have trouble sleeping, I simply remember this smell and it helps me go to sleep. I simply would also note, in my lifetime, the smell is the only thing I have ever felt had an addictive quality to it. I do fear the slight craving I feel for this drug's effect on my brain. I suppose I refer to this in regard to the loss of a very popular singing star, who may or may not have become overly familiar with using anesthesia to seek sleep. The bypass of normal taste and olfaction receptors, giving neuronal signals to the olfactory bulb, replaced by direct bloodstream insult, is a preliminary thought to that addictive urge I can sense even today. Such direct stimulation of brain centers, the thought of injected heroin, is not an experience mankind's evolutionary development can handle: danger and beware.

Once asleep, another agent—a muscle relaxant—is given to prevent injury during the seizure, as in a muscle pull or something similar. Depending on the patient, a mouth piece might also be inserted. The controlled impulse delivered to the patient is done at this center with a spECTrum 5000Q. The impulse can be delivered right unilateral, bi-frontal or bilateral. The settings are very multifactorial. Understand, typically a minimum of six treatments are necessary to be effective; six to twelve is the normal range. Sometimes maintenance sessions are required. It should be noted, certain psychotropic medications interfere with a successful therapeutic seizure, so the medications may need to be augmented or stopped. This is determined after a session of ECT. Some medications that inhibit the seizure are anti-anxiety medications, and some are mood stabilizers.

For completeness, I will note ECT is used for depression, dementia, catatonia, chemical imbalances and some types of autism (behavioral outbursts). Pregnant women suffering from depression might find ECT an option, avoiding antidepressants in their baby's bloodstream. During my re-visit to the hospital, I did explain to staff I was hopeful ECT would find applications in breaking the brain-lock cycle of OCD. But, as of 2014, I believe they had been unsuccessful in doing so.

I would awake groggy, tired and hungry from this session, as with others. Yes, I was head-achy, but this was not extreme by any means. It was fortuitous I did not suffer memory loss to the extent others do. At this time, without having researched or investigated reasons for this, I have no explanation. Physically, I do know I have a very thick skull; skull thickness is an important variable in charge settings and seizure creation. I'll leave this notation in here for my later research, fully aware of the ammunition being given to my comrades' sophomoric humor.

The best of friends bear best of quips, to make one look like a witless dimwit. RWL

Mr. Bruce Hornsby says it best: *That's just the way it is, some things will never change ...*

Fasting is necessary for the procedure. Post a seizure of the brain, upon awaking, it is amazing how delicious a peanut butter sandwich and a small pack of *Lorna Doones* can taste. One can expect a five to six-hour sleep post this procedure, and I was ECT symptom-free upon awakening the next day. I do not recall any memory loss the next day, but again, I believe this to be atypical.

The four major depressions I suffered during this thirty-one-year long ordeal, in my case, were of environmental origin. Medication relieved one, the other three were relieved by ECT. They were the result of life circumstances surrounding my OCD, the treatment of my OCD and the resulting theorized side effects and sequelae generated by the medications being used for treatment.

So yes, one might say these depressions were the indirect result of medication-induced psychiatric events of burnout and psychotics breaks that crippled life's progress. To repeat, the other illnesses I describe were repeated burnout periods of four to six weeks, including paranoia, hallucinations and psychotic breaks. If any of the above is confusing, all will be cleared up as you continue to read. I believe my theory will be validated by thirty-one years of evidence, and a clean bill of health for the last nine-plus years. Regardless, the methods for great health in *InfinitE/IQ* will sustain a lifetime.

Please understand, while I believe my only physiological decrement during this thirty-one-year ordeal to be a blip in neurochemistry during adolescence, if I were bipolar (as I was misdiagnosed), cyclothymic or schizophrenic—or held any other label of mental illness—that would be OK as well! I'm proud to claim a personal cure, but I'm damn proud to represent the one out of four individuals on this Earth who one day will succumb to mental illness.

Folks, the brain, like your blood vessels, your arms and legs, and your heart is part of the human body. Recognition of this mysterious entity residing atop our necks as being a physiological entity does not negate the concept of spirit.

I've said this before, but until the mentally ill receive the same understanding and empathy of a cancer patient, we all still have a long way to go. The good news is we will all get there. Keep reading. I hope the following pages enlighten and intrigue you.

Our next stop is back in time to the spring of 1982, when parental and personal desperation left me to enter the world of an experimental pharmacologic.

There is nothing wrong, but everything right with hope!

CHAPTER 14

GOING TO TRIAL, AND RELEASE FROM PRISON

I awoke this morning with clarity of thought and drive. A stroll down Old Indian Trail Road, once a pathway for the Lenape Indians across the valley, led me to the shores of beautiful Lake Wallenpaupack. In 1926, close to 3,000 men built a hydroelectric plant and cleared the path for this 5,700-acre recreational reservoir. I jumped into the lake in the early a.m., children asleep, and quiescent waters awaiting me. It was the Fourth of July, and a few laps along the fifty-two miles of wondrous shoreline would leave me refreshed, full of memories and eager to pen out a few words before shouts of eggs and blueberry pancakes emerged from the glow and glory of my wife and little girls.

The writing on ECT and anesthesia the day prior, and the eclipsing to unconsciousness, prompted me to throw the family into our vehicle and head north late yesterday afternoon. Our route: along Routes 22, 78, 287, 80, 15, 6, 84, 402 and 507. My girls directed me, and soon we would enter tranquility. Our goal: to catch the setting sun beneath the tree line across the one-mile breadth of the lake. Last night's sunset was even more spectacular than ever before, as stratus clouds hung just above the tree line, so the setting, bulbous fire generated spectacular purple hues across the skies. My little girls, now five and six years old, were no longer afraid of the vastness of the lake. They splashed about, as I pointed across the way. They left me to pen fearlessly this morning.

Emerging from the now-rippled waters, eyes in contact with the rising sun, I reflected as I walked back up Old Indian Trail Road. I thought about the brutal state of mind I was in when I was with my family on vacation at Lake Wallenpaupack the summer of 1979.

My OCD had just begun towards the beginning of the summer following freshman year, and now we were into August. My father and mother rented a small bungalow just a few miles down the shore-line from where they would eventually build their summer home in 1984. I remember it like it was yesterday. The pain of the obsessions had become brutal. I resorted to shaking my head, etch-a-sketch style, to remove the incessant redundant thoughts. I felt hot, sweaty, stressed and anxious every minute of every day. Grandma Irma, who I watched Yankee baseball with every night of prior summers, was not with us for this trip.

It was usually Yankee baseball, with the *Odd Couple* and the *Honeymooners* to follow on summer week nights. I would sit on Grandma's bed and watch Thurman swat to left and Sweet Lou drive opposite field to right. Felix and Oscar Madison would abuse each other later, and Ralph sent everyone to the moon around eleven p.m. I loved the *Odd Couple*, but if ever there was a show that misrepresented what OCD is about, it was this one. Felix's preoccupations, in black and white, revealed and drew smiles. But, in real life, the mind of a Felix, if OCD-diagnosed, would be one of pain and agony—this is the reality.

I recall walking into the cabin on a hot August day, the radio on, and the news flash of the crashing of Yankee catcher Thurman Munson's plane—reporting his death. A quick internet search reveals the date to be August 2, 1979. Tears rolled down my face that day, as an already miserable state of mind became frozen. It would be another three years and nine months, until March of 1982, before the monster and my imprisonment would be lifted.

And now, I am again forced to reflect on leaving North Carolina and the ride home with my father. You have to understand, I spent three years absorbed with this condition, at least in the context of human activity and life. Now I was coming home to a world of isolation, void of goals and without hope. I didn't have school or know what to tell friends, all dispersed post-high school, and brothers left perplexed and unknowing. As a human being, isolation is an ingredient for depression, and so the next few months of '81 into '82 became even more dreadful.

My parents, through their concern and diligence, became aware of an experimental drug trial on a pharmacologic, with indications of relief for obsessive-compulsive disorder, anorexia nervosa, bulimia nervosa and possibly others. The trial was to be double-blind in nature, defined as 50% of the individuals receiving the experimental drug—and the remainder the placebo—all unknowing the contents of the pill they ingested. I would be enrolled in March of 1982, having satisfied trial criteria. The location of the trial was the mental health facility in Belle Mead, New Jersey.

I, of course, hoped to receive this tricyclic antidepressant that had strong, yet non-selective serotonin reuptake inhibitor properties (SSRI), and not the placebo. The drug in development was originally thought to have exerted its therapeutic effect by inhibiting re-uptake of serotonin and norepinephrine (NE) of nerve cells. This action would be immediate, and yet trial results showed at least a two-week lag time to effects.

This led to the currently accepted modality of action. For semi-completeness, I will include its action below. Simply understand the end result is increased brain neurotransmitter noradrenaline and serotonin levels. The drug acts through receptor modification (sensitivity) in the cerebral cortex and the hippocampus. The exact protein target is the sodium-dependent serotonin transporters where the drug inhibits these three protein targets, where antagonist activity is noted: 5-hydroxytryptamine receptor 2A, 2B and 2C.

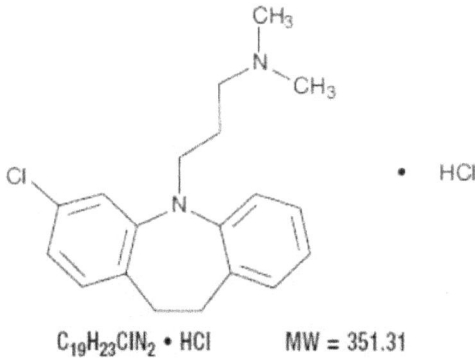

$C_{19}H_{23}ClN_2$ • HCl   MW = 351.31

Structural Formula of :

3-chloro-5-[3-(dimethylamino)propyl]-10,11-dihydro-
5H-dibenz[b,f] azepine monohydrochloride

Yes, other pharmacodynamics and mechanisms are in play. Interestingly enough, some sources cite an unknown mechanism of action. Please note: the drug does have non-selective action, naturally leading to the multiplicity of action.

In Chapter 15, I will elucidate what is theorized to be long-term receptor changes, leading to the therapeutic effect of the drug. Do not be alarmed at the complexity. Rather, marvel at the brain's design, including the methods of feedback and communication. Appreciate the vulnerability to the outside influence of medications, or even extreme dosing of natural products.

I walked into the professional atrium at the clinic, warmed and hopeful as I sat outside the office of Dr. Hornalle. Ceilings were high and potted plants abounded. I was greeted by the physician, and he explained the trial as he signed and checked off mounds of paper work. I used to love watching Dr. Hornalle work.

Picture a doctor with piles of paperwork on his desk, making checks and initials—picking up, penning and re-stacking papers at lightning-frenetic speed. By all means, I am not suggesting sloppy, unorganized or uncaring work. Rather, Dr. Hornalle was a maniac at work: perfect for his patients. His head even bobbed up and down at lightning speed, upon occasional eye contact. He sort of reminds me of myself in the healthy state, but in the OCD state, he almost became blurry—like mid-air, initialing confetti.

Dr. Hornalle was fascinating. He was the director of the Anorexia and Bulimia Unit, and—of course—you are beginning to see why my theory has overlap with these disorders.

Week One of the trial went by with no relief. Week Two also went by with no relief, and I became concerned. *Did I have the placebo?* When the drug finally reached F.D.A. approval in 1991, it was determined to have a 40 to 60% success rate. *If I were receiving the drug, would it even work?*

By Week Three, my enthusiasm waned as the doctor asked me the same series of questions. It seemed like one page held a single question, thus the piles, leading to the initialing frenzy and ensuring mayhem. I only hoped no one bought Dr. Hornalle any coffee, as I pondered the funneling of air and tornado effects within his being, office milieu and even the rain-forested atrium.

Week Four came and went, and I felt dejected.

Then, as Week Five approached, I was freed; I was released from prison. I'll never forget almost kissing and hugging the man, if I could catch him, when I entered his office on Week Five. The drug kicked in full-force four weeks into the trial.

It was absolute: one hundred percent elimination of symptoms. There was absolutely no gradual reduction of symptoms. I make mention of this to help the layman understand the uninterrupted personal nature of this disorder for me, incessant ruminations with one painful preoccupation, only to be replaced by another. I had not felt like myself for close to four years, except for my time in North Carolina. The obsessions were gone. Dr. Hornalle grinned and smiled from ear to ear, his head upright for at least twenty seconds in joy. My perspective on life would be changed forever. I cherished the moment as my morning reminder, every day forward. It is the origin of my opening, *A Letter to my Reader*:

Dear Reader,

When was the last time you took notice of young toddlers at play and witnessed the joy, love, innocence, fire for learning, void of inhibition and infinite energy they exude: a sight that just left you chuckling with a friend?

Or when was the last time you laid down on a forest floor on a cool summer's eve and listened to the canopy's opera of chattering birds, just prior to the silence that ensues when the sun finally sets, and nature grants permission to rest?

We're a species that certainly "enjoys" different viewpoints and manufacturers opinions—usually too quickly and in abundance—but I believe we all can agree our time on this rotating sphere we call home is finite. I can only hope after this read, you learn to live in the moment and enjoy this gift of life.

I can only hope you do not have to learn this lesson the hard way, as I did. I wish to find the courage to share with you a story, and open my heart, so my words flow smoothly and inspire, teach and make you thirst for more knowledge—and in life.

There is nothing wrong, yet everything right and wonderful with hope.

I should note the usage of this tricyclic drug did have one side effect that was frustrating: difficulty—to the degree of near impossibility—in having an orgasm and, of course, to in turn ejaculate. It would be a problem that would exist until 1991—almost a decade. Yes, I was going to write a separate chapter called *Come Again*, but I do have some level of impulse control.

I was nineteen years old with the trial underway. I had lived the majority of my adolescence in misery, and had six months left until my twentieth birthday. A new beginning could indeed be my only glass-full outlook.

With the pain of North Carolina still fresh, and the clinical trial being in New Jersey, I sought admission to a state university in New Jersey. Matriculation at this university was set for the fall of 1982.

Open your heart, and let your emotions paint the pages with words of passion, inspiration and knowledge!

CHAPTER 15

COME AGAIN, SIDE EFFECTS AND EVOLUTION

April Fools?

In Chapter 14, I indicated I had no intention of discussing the difficulty in achieving orgasm on the 1982 clinical trial drug that bought relief. With no quandary on having a discussion on impulse control, and an absolute embracing of the joy of fun, let's have a chat about ejaculation.

I can only ask the reader, "If you had a ten-year *drought* in orgasms and ejaculations, wouldn't you want to know why?"

Kidding aside, in this chapter I'd like to deviate slightly from my plan of simple medical explanations and delve a little deeper, and with more detail, for three purposes:

1) The detail below will exhibit the complexity of the brain.
2) The description of evolution will highlight the sensitivity of the neurology and biochemistry of the body.
3) To provide background for *The Lindemann Theory*, leading to my ultimate cure and the benefits for you in utilizing *InfinitE/IQ*.

Again, do not be alarmed at the complexity. Rather, embrace and marvel at the brain's design, methods of feedback and communication, and appreciation of vulnerability to medications, or even extreme dosing of natural products.

In Chapter 14, I promised a bit more detail on the mechanism of action of the pharmacologic that resolved my OCD. I would first like to explain that when a drug is taken and enters the bloodstream, the actual active metabolites exert their therapeutic effect -those metabolites determined by enzymatic systems of chemical breakdown.

For example, unbeknownst to me, the experimental drug I was given—now widely used in western Europe—is metabolized into demethylclomipramine. The parent and this product are hydroxylated to metabolites, which are further conjugated before excretion in urine. The cytochrome P450 is responsible for the parent drug breakdown and the metabolite. Some patients who did not respond to the drug, with a 40-60% success rate, may have been genetically deficient in the hydroxylation mechanism (P450). The result would be accumulations of high amounts of dimethyl-clomipramine, with possibly no effect and/or serious side effects.

One can only wonder today if genetic analysis is being utilized, or could be utilized, to examine that P450 system, in relation to prescribed medications and their breakdown? In 1982 and today, genetic analysis would be an obvious prerequisite to enter the trial: good for patient, pharmaceutical company and FDA approval. It would benefit healthcare system costs and efficacy, and be great for medicine.

A quick summary: the drug that enters the bloodstream may not be the chemical compound when it finally hits its target. If an individual is missing a piece of chemistry, that could affect the final result: no result, or even worse, the introduction of a deleterious chemical.

As a quick analogy: we're baking yeast breads today. We add sugar, salt and oil to two bowls of flour. Unaware to the baker, one of the bowls of flour contains a product of flour with built-in yeast, while the other simply has flour. When the bread comes out of the oven, it is discovered the missing piece of yeast has created an unhappy loaf of bread.

Let's examine the mechanism of action of tricyclic medications in general, after they typically reach the steady state, after three weeks in the body. Hang in there, everyone. We get selective inhibition of the NE and serotonin (5-HT) synapses. Receptors at beta and alpha-2 adrenoceptors are depressed, whereas 5-HT receptors are enhanced. Responses at alpha-1 adrenoceptors and 5-HT receptors remain unchanged. Thus, post-synaptic flow at NE and 5-HT will be reduced through beta-adrenoceptors, but enhanced via 5-HT receptors. Keep in mind, although alpha-1 adrenoceptors remain unchanged, the likely action is post-synaptic travel would be enhanced. In effect, desensitization of alpha-2 adrenoceptors will provide greater communication of synaptic NE, to activate normosensitive postsynaptic alpha-1 adrenoceptors. The result is more 5-HT and NE in the neuronal synapses.

As another analogy, you're on the shores of Lake Mead with the Hoover Dam at the end. If you skip two rocks a certain way, a round one and a triangular one, the dam opens. Now, if the circle stone bounces off the head of a lake trout and hits a fallen maple tree, thus impeding the flight of the skipped triangular stone and causing deflection to the head of a fly fisherman, then a floating human body to the claws of hell of the dam activates an alarm, sending emergency personnel to give the gent a free pass to the roller coaster Colorado River below. LOL. My apologies, my reader, I have no simple analogy. Rather, we have learned about receptors and communication in the wondrous brain, and between—its incredible neuronal network.

Point made, the brain is complex. Just remember, in the brain and the rest of the body, receptors exist. They can be acted upon in a variety of ways that effect communications. And there are checks on these communications that have consequences on other chemical, neurological and hormonal chemistries. It is an extremely well-organized, intricate and interdependent system with a very long and divergent timeline. The lesson learned: if you are going to augment the chemistry, be careful—very careful. Side effects are an obvious, and almost imminent, byproduct.

The neurological and biochemical systems of the human body have a very long and divergent timeline. Eicosanoids are an extremely significant class of proto-hormones in humans, first discovered in 1936. They represent the first hormonal system of living organisms, having evolved some 500 million years ago. These hormones control all systems above and communicate between cells. Primates diverged from mammals some 85 million years ago. Humans diverged some 5.5 million years ago. In essence, one could really say the human body's chemistry has been evolving for 500 million years, although we usually settle for the 5.5 million years as modern man's development. As a perspective of the vastness of 5.5 million years, let us just take a twenty-year period of life and denote it represents just .00036364 % of human evolutionary time.

We conclude biological and neuronal chemistry have a balance with many checks and feedback mechanisms, all of which are under the same evolutionary constraints and have evolved with particular types of fuel (food). That conclusion leaves us with one final reminder of the delicate and complex balance we are working with: the introduction of foreign substances.

Pharmaceutical and other biologically active substances are an important and necessary component of medicine, but the very complexity and balance I spoke of above is the reason my illness was protracted another twenty-seven years. Understand, these substances are a necessity at times, with the goal of a return to uninterrupted chemistry being the desire.

The motto should be: *Proceed with Hope and Caution.*

Our slogan to be: *Achieve Health and Remove Barriers to Restore Health, if Possible.*

Okay, I know it is killing you. Why is it difficult to have an orgasm and ejaculate while on this and similar medications? The two processes, orgasm and male ejaculation, have two separate mechanisms of activation, physiologically speaking. Both are very complex and depend on many hormonal systems. It is known serotonin 5-HT does inhibit activation, per ejaculation. It is known drugs that inhibit 5-HT reuptake, such as the one I was taking, impair ejaculation. Thus, it is used medically for premature ejaculation. The effect does occur in the brain. It is known that, in the spine, serotonin will enhance the process of ejaculation. So yes, if so inclined, sever your spine and a little dab will do you. Disclaimer: *Please don't do this*!

For completeness, understand there are fourteen receptor subtypes for 5-HT. Subtypes 1A, 1B and 2C are involved with ejaculation. I will assume, for brevity at this time, that while achieving orgasm and ejaculation have two separate mechanisms, 5-HT is involved with both. Thus, both have overlapping mechanisms and hormonal systems as well.

So, the moral of the story is, if you're a guy, cherish this trio (1A, 1B and 2C). If you're a gal, understand that if you "Inhibit the three, you will ride long and worry-free." Not sure you will see this on any pharmaceutical commercials soon though? Imagine that jingle?

One last and very important note for me and others as well. While investigating my experimental drug during this writing, I discovered that during premarketing testing, hypomania and mania were precipitated in several patients. Also, the same was seen in tricyclic medications that have similar properties. The following side effects were also noted: delusions, hallucinations, psychotic episodes, confusion and paranoia. Believe it or not, this is the first time I have been made aware of this. This all concerns me greatly. Actually quite devastating, as I most likely would have figured my cure much earlier, and avoided the kidney damage caused by the misdiagnosis, not to mention a halt to quite a bit of pain and suffering.

I should note, I did not experience these side effects with this medication, but rather another side effect. My concern comes from two other medications, one of which was a combination of drugs I was later prescribed that did create these symptoms. Those two regimens were used to treat my OCD and created—in my theory—not just mania-type symptoms, but long-term-burnout symptoms as well, indirectly causal for depression. My angst concerning the creation of these side effects would be future misdiagnosis, the pre-scribing of new medications to treat the unexplained side effects, the protraction of the ordeal to thirty-one years and being forced to abandon my dream of becoming a physician post a near sixteen-year tenure of schooling.

Validation for my claim of medication-induced effects comes from nine-plus years of symptom-free living, upon my development of *The Lindemann Theory* and utilization of *InfinitE/IQ* to replace medication, restoring a natural neurochemical milieu. The result is a brain alive with energy, creativity and analytical reasoning—re-stored and boundless, and a vibrant neurochemical network, learn-ing through dendritic expansion and limiting neuronal destruction.

So, we leave this chapter with an insight and respect for balance, and a desire to keep it and improve the brain upon its foundation. Keep reading, I have a recipe to maintain health and reach peak per-formance. The foundation of my history is being laid wide open, and it will become evident how my conclusions were reached and how health was achieved. I'm bearing my life open for the betterment of your own—I hope it works.

There is nothing wrong, but everything right with hope!

CHAPTER 16

THE WOW FACTOR: IT'S A WONDERFUL THING

I just perused a neurobiology book of well over 500 pages, detailing the human brain. The author's epilogue begins by describing the entire text as only a vague summary of the vastness of knowledge that exists and will exist on this remarkable structure—the human brain and consciousness.

The text clearly surmises what I understand and believe essential to a state of health and longevity for the human being. The brain requires stress, activity and thinking to prosper, just as the body requires exercise and stress to excel and develop. Just as intense muscular activation arouses dormant stem cells, which respond by generating new actin and myosin filaments—and in turn "new muscles"—the DNA template in the brain requires the challenges of good stress to activate neuronal nerve endings to begin sprouting and connecting: a dendritic explosion. The concept of stress, response and adaptation is ubiquitous throughout the human body. Generate new muscle and new blood vessels and nervous system connections will follow.

So, do your crossword puzzles. Employers: challenge your employees. Activate your genetic DNA to RNA. Watch enzymes build, which in turn produces proteins, macromolecules and new spouts and synapses. Treat your brain like a vegetable and you will invite transneuronal degeneration, much as the dormant endurance athlete of even two weeks begins to suffer detraining.

The happy human being recipe has just started.

Rule #1:

Challenge yourself and enjoy the rewards.

The brain is an absolutely wondrous entity, with a wow factor coming from the step forward and beyond other mammalian brains we know. That leap includes our ascent to language, vast memory capacities, massive problem-solving and creativity capabilities, and most uniquely: a relationship to culture and consciousness.

Our 1.5 kg/3.3 lb. brains are highly developed, with the human cerebrum containing ten billion neurons, 400 million which sit in the primary visual cortex alone. Whales have brains five times the size of ours, dolphin's brain size exceeds ours, and cats are maybe one-fifth the size of ours. While these mammals all exhibit tremendous intelligence, our dense packing and arrangements have allowed us to feel a "me".

With this said, I have a secret confession. I grew up with a cat in the house, and sometimes I felt he had us all fooled. He somehow arranged to have a chair and placemat at the dinner table, managed to bring the heads of small creatures to the front steps and receive applauds, and even served as my father's alarm clock each morning—gently raising his brow to say hello. Keep this to yourselves, but that cat had an eerie intelligence about him.

The study of the brain can be broken down into multiple categories. This will include molecular neurobiology, neurogenetics, neuropharmacology, neuromathematics, neurocommunication and neurochemistry. If anyone has an "in" to my word-processing program, please let them know these words are spelled correctly and to stop throwing red underlines upon them; get with the program.

Don't worry, folks, I'll get to the chapter on the explosion of technology, and we can't keep up with that explosion of technology. As if in the last twenty years, evolution has broadened the scope of our intellect, yet the wonders of our code leave our neurons to degenerate with app after app of listless viewing. Five hundred million years of hormonal evolution, folks, to refine the three pounds atop our head, and yet Silicone Valley has replaced evolution. Huh! Do the math: twenty years of 500 million is .000004% of our development. Get a grip.

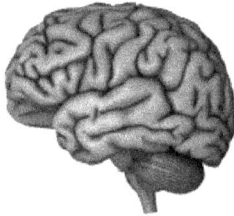

The truth, and the absolute truth is, if education keeps cutting physical education and our children remain sedentary, eating high-glycemic foods, saturated fats, and farmed-out proteins, and computer visuals re-pattern our cerebrums, we will be in de-evolution, yes de-evolution! Teachers, challenge my daughters' minds, and administrators keep reading on: clean fuel, challenging exercise—physical and mental—and community create the foundation to build on.

The experimental drug I was taking is said to act on the cerebral cortex and the hippocampus. A simple review of these two structures is presented here. The cerebral cortex has evolved as the most recent of all the brain structures and exhibits the largest variation in terms of adaptation. The existing theories on cortical evolution both have their origin with stem-cell differentiation. The cerebral cortex allows for cognition, awareness, thought, language, consciousness, memory, attention and perception.

It is the very essence of this entity that allowed me to perform a retrospective analysis of my case history, develop a hypothesis and carry out the healthy lifestyle of the hypothesis; thereby testing the hypothesis, and subsequently describing and exploring the cure I believe has world-wide application, if not consideration. *The Lindemann Theory* and *InfinitE/IQ* have left me medication free and nine-plus years symptom free—alive, thriving and prepared to spread the word.

The scientific method includes two paths: gather data and create a hypothesis, or create a hypothesis and gather evidence. The former was not an option, the latter saved my life. From an idea comes a cure, from a cure comes the release of "me" and "you". From the awareness of a society comes a desire to share with you my story. Read on, and I will help set you and me free.

One cortical-mapping scheme of the cerebral cortex's neocortex (90% of the cortex) reveals fifty-one different areas. This scheme is described to reveal the complexity once again. Genetic analysis has shown a neocortical evolutionary link to mushroom bodies within ragworms that existed as far back as the Precambrian Era, 4.6 billion years ago. Wow, that's a bit further back than even 500 million years!

The good news is our twenty-year .000004% just went to an even lower percent. The bad news: the very seat of our intelligence has genetic roots to a worm, and a ragworm at that. This is the type of information that needs to be stored in a vault of some sort. Perhaps I should hit delete?

We'll move on.

The hippocampus is a component of the brain's limbic system and has important roles in consolidation of data from short-term to long-term memory, and in spatial memory, which provides navigation. It is an area of the brain with a plethora of different cell types, and where a process called long-term potentiation (the way memories are stored) was first discovered. The brain has a hippocampus in each of our two cerebral hemispheres. Many researchers feel memory function is correlated with the median temporal lobe, part of the cerebral cortex described above.

Please note: the hippocampus contains high levels of glucocorticoid receptors, and thus is very vulnerable to stress and the hormone released during stress, cortisol. This sentence is extremely important, as it becomes part of my theory in why certain sequelae (other symptoms created by meds) developed to protract and confuse my illness. My theory contends the very thoughts of OCD are so powerfully stress generating, cortisol release becomes toxic to hippocampal neurons and perhaps other brain structurers, maintaining the brainlock. The power of the lock can make the condition nonresponsive to traditional psychotherapy and behavioral techniques.

Evidence points to the fact that dendritic sprouting and restoration will occur when stress is removed. Also, the hippocampus is one of the few brain regions where new neurons are generated, which can be positively effected by exercise. Please note the importance of exercise here! And, of course, this coupled with the fact exercise and healthy eating reduces cortisol levels is exciting. Exercise and healthy eating expands the recipe for hippocampal and life health restoration.

We will continue to explore the brain along the way, but let me reiterate briefly some key points made above.

- A marvelous design, the brain loves positive stress, thinking, problem solving and debate.

- A sedentary brain pulls back neuronal connections.
- Chronic stress, the type producing cortisol, has deleterious effects, particularly in the hippocampus.
- Exercise promotes neuronal growth in the hippocampus and reduces cortisol, thereby reducing hippocampal damage.
- Proper fuel, described in detail in subsequent chapters, reduces cortisol—among many other benefits—thereby reducing chances of hippocampal damage.

And finally, cortisol reduction is a central component of my theory in finding a cure.

We have the basis for the rest of the story. There will be some scary pieces to follow, but in conflict and confusion, resolution was achieved. Whether you are afflicted with OCD and want relief, or you simply want to enjoy this life to the fullest, please read on and enjoy every minute of every day. When you arise with the rising sun, go ahead and shout, "Today is going to be my best day yet!"

Open your heart, and let your emotions paint the pages with words of passion, inspiration and knowledge!

CHAPTER 17

RABID ANIMALS AND THE UNFORGETTABLE

Last night I awoke at three a.m., eyes wide open. My wife, Rosanne, fast asleep—Rhaena and Rochelle asleep as well. My two youngsters, as usual, were very unappreciative of their mattress' north-south longitudinal design, one choosing a perpendicular line, the other upside down and all around. When this text is complete, I certainly will look at market size for my new design: the sided, circular mattress. Isn't that a cage?

Have I had any caffeine all day? I do my best to keep away from this member of the xanthine family of drugs. I know it has an average clearance of ten hours, but with this said, it can range from three to nineteen hours. And, as I spoke about active metabolites in Chapter 14, caffeine is converted to paraxanthine in the body. This active chemical hangs around longer than caffeine, so the above clearance numbers are inconsequential anyway. No, as I recall, no caffeine yesterday.

Huh, you know what, it was time to use the restroom; that's why I awoke. As we continue my story, you will discover I was eventually misdiagnosed. I was placed on a medication called lithium carbonate, and I believe it was for a period of about ten years. Unfortunately, as my theory unfolds, you will realize there was no need for this medication. And fortunately, the only residual effect from this thirty-one-year ordeal—and let's not forget the ordeal itself—was that this drug damaged my kidneys. The damage is thankfully non-progressive, but nonetheless the drug created the condition of nephrogenic diabetes insipidus.

Specifically, the drug damaged basal lamina cells in the collecting tubules of my kidney, thus causing a deficit in the concentration of urine. I do get to check on all my beautiful girls each night a bit more than the normal being.

Simply put, I must drink a lot of water and urinate very frequently, and that urine being very dilute explains my necessary constant thirst and intake of water. While a medication does exist to remedy this, I understand the target chemistry is involved in other reactions throughout the body, not specific to the kidneys; thus, my choice to avoid it. I did take the medication once, and sensed a detraction in my motivation and drive. Again, this was an observation I chose not to investigate or further validate with continued use. As long as man keeps planting trees, I will be okay. Yes, of course I am tempted to quip about the tune, "Tie a Yellow Ribbon Round the Old Oak Tree", but please?

In any event, I was awake at three a.m.. Understanding how important sleep is to regenerating the myelin sheathing (nerve insulation) in my brain, I chose to walk the neighborhood, seeking fatigue to get back to sleep. The cool summer eve left me to chuckle as I remembered a recent visit to an orthopedist's office: my six-year-old being treated for a buckle fracture of the wrist. Upon departure from the office, I noticed hanging a full-length, three-foot skeletal model of a human being. The model's cranium was half-removed, leaving me to jest with the receptionist.

Yes, I too was affected by Sir Anthony Hopkins and the 2001 thriller *Hannibal.* I watched the character Krendler enjoying his dinner, folds of his cerebral hemispheres shimmering in the lights, while Dr. Lecter dissects, sauté, and feeds the smiling gent his prefrontal cortex. You know, I read Hopkins chose this movie because of its dialog. I also read the critics had mixed reviews. All I know is that in terms of my recent description of long-term potentiation, the mixed reviews may have been because the scene left most of us as damaged goods.

I was thus propelled into memories of Jeff Goldblum and *The Fly*, and his 1986 portrayal of Seth Brundle, a telepod-genetics enthusiast. On the big screen, I watched Seth studying himself in a mirror, while he metamorphosed into a fly as required artifacts were removed from his face in a hellish, never-ending scene. Never had I experienced acting that expressed and drawed within me fear, empathy, compassion, sardonic wit and intrigue as Seth removed his facial cartilage, lips, nose, ears and the rest—and quipped about placing them in a museum somewhere. Goldblum must have had a fly under a microscope for days.

I guess what I'm trying to express is, Jeff and Sir Anthony, did you have to do such a good job of acting? And so, my walk proceeded and I was through pondering plated brains and morphing humans. I was reminded of a very not-so-funny story. Let me tell you this story. The story scared me, my family, and hospital personnel. The story was life-threatening.

He was in a room, a cage, in lockdown. The being was no longer human, transformed by overages of a substances, leaving the very brain chemical harmony described previously not just in disarray—but in total chaos. The human neurotransmitters bathed in mayhem, the body in full fight-or-flight mode, as adrenaline pushed for escape.

While the room seemed stable or secure, the door was not steel. The door hinges, perhaps, the wrong grade of steel. Perhaps the only thing that saved all was the fact the runway path to the door was short, at most ten feet.

It makes me shiver to describe the night. He wanted out. Hospital personnel, unprepared for zoo-like conditions, wanted him in. These folks would need no caffeine to stay awake this night. He vaguely remembers the place, but thinks he knows its name and location. Is it worth validating his memory, he would later ask? And so, it happened. He ran full speed, leveled shoulder and linebacker-style attacked the door. He retreated and prepared for the next launch. He could hear frantic shouts and cries outside the wired-in window of the door. Someone braced against the door.

Again, he slammed the door, after a full sprint, reversing the impacting shoulder. The door splintered. Cries and wales erupted again, and the outer bracing went to three or four people, with cries for more bodies. Determined, he attacked again. This time the upper hinge broke free.

He attacked again; the bottom hinge was shattered. The door was now free-floating, held in the air by six or seven external bodies. He remembers pain, sweat and dirt. He remembers sirens, alarms and screams. And with chaos he retreated, and attacked again and again and again, and then he collapsed and remembers no more. When he awoke, he was no longer there.

He was me. The event lasted fifteen minutes. The year was 1983. I will get to what happened as the story continues to unfold.

There is nothing wrong, but everything right with hope!

CHAPTER 18

A YEAR OF LIFE

Almost four years of absolute agony ended after entering the experimental drug protocol at the Belle Mead, New Jersey Mental Health Facility. Certainly, the four to six weeks in North Carolina were a blessing, but when the hammer fell and the blessing became mixed, the plunge into despair was only magnified, leaving me isolated from society.

The brain receptor changes that ensued over the first four weeks of the drug trial removed the obsessions, and allowed matriculation to one of New Jersey's finest universities in the fall of 1982 and the spring of 1983.

Oddly enough, I grew up just fifteen minutes up the road from the New Brunswick campus. Even after graduation, and actually not until the last ten years, did I realize what a fantastic reputation this university had per academia and quality of graduates. Classes, coursework and studies were rigorous, but I enjoyed the fall, spring and a summer classes. I was able to do quite well and complete the likes of biology, chemistry, expository writing, microeconomics, calculus for engineers, analytical physics and an introduction to experimentation.

While I pondered biomedical engineering, I really was uncertain as to the career path I was on. Lack of planning—well after you read the upcoming chapters, you might conclude I was trying to survive. My eventual completion of degrees in biology and psychology with honors were by no means in anticipation of even a notion of entering medical school. Had my early goal been the latter, I by no means would have taken the difficult courses and achieved an even better GPA, than I did while attaining my degrees; nonetheless, the difficult courses were extremely preparatory. I was simply trying to stay grounded and alive again that first year, and get in the groove again. The desire to pursue medicine, because of my interests, would seem to have been an obvious choice. Yet, the goal was not set until after a very funny and intriguing interview out of college. I will explain later.

My father and two brothers were electrical engineers, but the path towards medicine might have been an obvious on, when I consider the time I spent in the bowels of the library at the University of Medicine and Dentistry of New Jersey Rutgers' campus. It was during my junior year of high school, aged seventeen, in a class called methods of research, when I decided to research and eventually write a fifty-page paper on immunology. I am going to describe this to you, because this research and subsequent paper represented the most frustrating and humiliating obsession of them all.

The topic of immunology was fascinating to me, but I made one clear mistake. If there ever was a topic you wanted to pick up an introductory paragraph on, it would be this one. In the human body, you have what is called cell-mediated immunity and humoral immunity. Going into a library with hundreds of books on each subject, unaware of these two branches—while seeking unity—became frustrating. I also spent hours going through microfiche. The folks at the library were great. My brain was already in overload, and the project became arduous. The results were spectacular: a very happy teacher and a grade of 115.

Here's the killer.

The obsession became relentless: I never had a clear, absolute understanding of the subject. Part of my brain wanted to me to speak to the teacher and ask for a lower grade; the other was like, *Are you off your rocker?* Now, this doesn't even touch on the subject of, *Your teacher will think you are off your rocker.* At least this obsession had a *touch* of reality to it though.

A couple weeks after the start of the obsession, and wanting this non-stop ritual out of my brain, I did just that: asked the teacher for a lower grade, despite months of research. Yes, he did it for me, but he looked at me with genuine concern—and rightfully so. A new obsession came in instantly. I'd killed another fence post. Those years were frightful. Rational thought and control were out of reach. The stress, pain, anxiety, exhaustion and heat were unrelenting and suffocating.

The obsessions were now gone, and my first collegiate year was complete. The summer of 1983 was underway. With a year at the university under my belt, my life was on track, and the nightmare was behind me. I'd already chosen classes for '83 and '84. The family home on Winthrop Road's white shingles and blue shudders looked a bit faded that summer. New beginnings warrant a new coat of paint. I painted the house, and that is when it happened. It would happen more than a dozen more times over the next twenty-five years: every time ruining my life, complicating diagnoses, recruiting more medications and leaving others speculating as to intentions I can only question.

The day after the painting project, I felt strange. I was exhausted—beyond exhausted: an exhaustion where I could not push myself further, when I always could. I simply thought a day in bed would suffice. I didn't make much of it, but again it had a strange and unfamiliar quality, this state of being.

I awoke the next morning, and I felt the same. I spent another day in bed. Again, let me stress, it was beyond tired or exhaustion. I felt a major life drain, almost a repulsion to activity, and an inability to push myself. There actually was a cognitive feeling that pushing through it, if possible, would be even more damaging. I described it to my parents as a burnout. I'm not sure where the term originated from, I just verbalized what I felt.

This state of being lasted about two or more weeks, and left my doctor and parents confused, though not overly concerned. After all, they just felt I was tired, but I knew this to be a wrong conclusion. One day I awoke, and I was back to my old energetic self. For clarity, it was not a gradual return of energy. It was as if a switch was put back in place: from no energy, back to complete energy. Dismissing the severity of it, and with no clarity on causation, I went on with the summer. In fact, no clarity was reached until 2009, when *The Lindemann Theory* was born.

Then, just weeks before my second-year fall semester at university was to begin, the obsessions came back full force—absolutely without reason. As with the scenario in North Carolina, I was devastated and frightened. *How could the medication just stop working?*

Did I accidently get switched to the placebo? Was there a manufacturing flaw, a change in drug formulation? Did the receptors lose sensitivity to the drugs? Did my doctor check a wrong box? Was I given the wrong bottle? Was the actual medication placed in a placebo bottle? It just seemed incomprehensible that a drug could miraculously eliminate symptoms for about fifteen months, and then without reason, conflict or anything—just give me anything—for some reason, a full-force return of OCD. Another switch, another nightmare, became the running theme.

Dr. Hornalle was also without explanation and perplexed, as was the drug company. Everything was on track in life—and again, suddenly taken away. I retreated in agony, and asked my father to withdraw me from classes, unsure of the medical explanation he gave to school administrators. As I write today, I can now offer a more scientific plausible reason for the drug cessation of efficacy, based on what I know and have theorized. Yet, I still am at a loss at what happened. As for the burnouts, the revelation I had per causation eight years ago is the reason I am now symptom-free. That explanation will appear in upcoming chapters.

I continued to take the experimental drug as September rolled around, but my parents began to worry at a mental state that was now not only pain, but spiraling to an abyss. North Carolina was gone, baseball was gone, and my dreams and goals were wiped away. New Jersey academics were gone. And what do you tell friends and other family members? The pain was not gone: sheer metal pain, anguish and exhaustion were not gone. The ruminating about the absurd wasn't gone, and I held no control over stopping it.

The isolation would take its toll. The beast against the barricade— was it imminent? And so, my parents responded. New options, new doctors, new shots, new pills, new hospitals, new opinions and mayhem were in suit. And then, two lines from the 1980 song "Games People Play", the lyrics by the Alan Parsons Project, began to ring in my head.

I don't wanna live here no more,
I don't wanna stay,
Ain't gonna spend the rest of my life,
Quietly fading away.

Despite the ringing and revolving thoughts, the pain, and the conflict and despair, I fought on to Chapter 19. Yes, Chapter 19 is going to be tough to write: thirty-plus years later, let me paint the pages ...

Open your heart, and let your emotions paint the pages with words of passion, inspiration and knowledge!

CHAPTER 19

THE SHADOW OF DEATH

As I departed down our driveway this morning, my daughters playing enthusiastically in the back seat. I took notice of the American flag jutting from the front door, and the half-round stars and stripes vintage bunting hanging from the detached garage's peak—displayed for Flag and Independence Day, which had just past. I am feeling a bit patriotic during this summer of 2017, and have chosen to let the two fly for the remainder of the summer, maybe even into the burnt orange, reds and yellows of the fall.

My wife and I were married on Flag Day, June 14, and just several weeks earlier than now we celebrated our ninth anniversary. Those flags reminded me of some advice I had asked Pastor Geo to read at our wedding in 2008.

Actually, the advice came from this guy a couple of thousand years ago, as he strolled up a hill, rising out of the Sea of Galilee. He explained to the crowd the following messages. History says it was a crowd, so I gather they valued his words. They went like this:

"Therefore, I tell you, do not worry about your life, what you will eat or drink; or about your body, what you will wear. Is not life more than food, and the body more than clothes?

Look at the birds of the air; they do not sow or reap or store away in barns, and yet your heavenly Father feeds them. Are you not much more valuable than they?

Can any one of you by worrying add a single hour to your life?

And why do you worry about clothes? See how the flowers of the field grow. They do not labor or spin."

And so, on my wedding day I wanted to share and remind myself again what I had learned during my ordeal. Live, enjoy and love in the moment.

And in turn, I was reminded of my father, Robert E. Lindemann. The baseball-sized tumor growing in his bladder on our wedding day was already seeking outside blood vessels in his body to spread its insidious, malignant attack. The folks at Robert Wood Johnson did their best against this squamous cell carcinoma. His kidney function precluded him from experimental chemotherapy cocktails, and his body for the next thirteen months—as have others—welcomed hope in the way of chemotherapeutic agents. The agents were perhaps archaic against these human-cell biologic mimics, a mimic with no timetable to die.

My wife and I visited Dad, and with Mom endured a night from hell on July 18, 2009. The a.m. hours were filled with projectile vomiting of blood, blood-filled carpets, screams of panic and a horrific argument with a hospice support group we were using. I was unaware they had no night hours. I laid in his blood, and cried like a baby on the carpet floor below his feet. The family was present when dad died around ten that morning. My tear ducts were empty by then, and I was thankful his pain was gone. He would not see the birth of either of our daughters, Rhaena or Rochelle. Rochelle asks often now, "Where is grandpa?" We tell her, and she always tells us she misses him. Indeed, we do too.

Pastor Geo eloquently recited this psalm a few day later, as he described the visual my father liked most, that of his savior holding a lamb in one hand and a staff in the other.

The Lord is my shepherd, I shall not want.

He makes me lie down in green pastures, He leads me beside still waters, He restores my soul. He guides me in paths of righteousness for His name's sake. Even though I walk through the valley of the shadow of death, I will fear no evil, for You are with me; Your rod and Your staff, they comfort me. You prepare a table before me in the presence of my enemies. You anoint my head with oil; my cup overflows. Surely goodness and love will follow me all the days of my life, and I will dwell in the house of the Lord forever. Amen.

And so, I hope he is with me as I write the remainder of this Chapter 19, "The Shadow of Death", and I retain the courage to pen and distribute this book for my fellow man.

My father understood the abyss his son was falling into upon semester withdrawal in the fall of 1983. I'm sure the failure of the experimental drug frightened him also. His research for the next cure took him to the Princeton University area, in search of another answer to a very perplexing problem. Imagine having a child consumed and unable to control the ridiculous. As a parent now, I can feel what that sense of dread must have felt like. It must have been horrific.

Biofeedback was introduced to us as a helpful modality for OCD therapy. It revolved around using peaceful cassette tapes, flowing streams and waterfalls to reduce biologic feedback such as pulse, blood pressure, skin temperature and other. The biofeedback sessions were unsuccessful.

Before I proceed further, I want to remind the reader I was still taking the trial drug during the fall of 1983, despite the fact it lost effectiveness. As of this writing, it would have seemed prudent to have come off the medication, in the hopes desensitization were the cause of failure. A resumption of the drug after being off it might again provide therapeutic value. I can only assume at this time that this was considered back then, but it could not be done because of clinical drug-trial protocol.

My father became aware of a Dr. Ham, who was known in the Princeton area as an orthomolecular psychiatrist. While I remained on the experimental drug, her theory was one of naturopathic medicine. Her regiment of therapy included a drink of green leaves in the morning and what seemed to be twenty to thirty pills of vitamins, amino acids and minerals every day. My hair would be analyzed for trace elements and other testing was performed.

What is intriguing is at the time, I felt the doctors' medicinal theory to be ludicrous; albeit, I was compliant. The theory was to use natural means to manipulate my body neurochemistry. I, by no means feel this way at all today. I do feel natural therapy will not be successful in breaking the OCD lock cycle, but once the cycle is broken, natural means can and should maintain health. I will elaborate later on the how and why of this.

One of the supplements I was taking was the essential amino acid tryptophan. Low levels of serotonin are associated with OCD causation and depression. With this said, both conditions are multifactorial in regard to origin. The basic premise of the large doses of tryptophan are that serotonin is derived from this amino acid, in the following simplified chemical pathway:

Tryptophan ➜ 5-Hydroxytryptophan ➜ Serotonin ➜ Melatonin

Please understand, this metabolism is extremely complex. Also, Tryptophan has a second major metabolic pathway in the human body. That is in the synthesis of kynurenine, and this pathway actually consumes 90% of tryptophan metabolism. Kynurenine precedes the making of kynurenic acid, which is an antagonist at glutamate ionotropic receptors. Now understand, there is strong evidence associating kynurenines with behavioral and cognitive symptoms of neurological disease. Also understand, in chemical reactions there are enzymes that are rate-limiting (they may or may not be protective), another factor to consider—perhaps in a later writing. With this said, the full effects of less or more tryptophan on metabolic pathways is not clear; nor is supportive or unsupportive, per elevating serotonin to therapeutic levels.

Again, I am simply making the point here: when you supplement with very high doses of precursors, the chemistry may not be specific. Also, even if tryptophan were specific to serotonin metabolism, and increases of 5-HT occurred, regulation of the addition in the brain plasma is complex. It is simply not good enough to look at the basics of biochemistries, especially when the specifics exist. With this stated, it may in fact be dangerous. The fact is Dr. Ham's regiment had no effect in preventing my obsessions. There was no decrease of symptoms.

Our next step was a clinic in Pennsylvania, where I was introduced to a Dr. Posnik. He was also a naturopathic doctor. I became a full-time patient at this clinic, receiving vitamin B-12 injections, placed under a machine daily with some type of restorative radiation and given healthy meals. I even had an iridology exam, another alternate form of medicine where the iris of my eyes was examined for clues to my illness etiology.

I was here with one other patient. She was a wonderful gal who suffered with a phobia of job interviews. She had completed her work as a special education language teacher, I believe, and was petrified to the point of phobia over interviewing for a career position.

The nights were isolating at this clinic, and I was losing faith in the methods of treatment. The people were wonderful, but even one of the nurses oddly told me I should not be there—not a real boost in confidence.

I had lost track of friends, don't recall speaking to my brothers, and was in the woods in Pennsylvania receiving B-12 injections, sunning in alien pods and consuming bean sprouts atop very grainy bread. I was losing hope, but what I was uncertain of, was how fast. And then it happened.

I was about to settle to bed one night. And then a plunge, the same plunge I would have years later when I felt driven to escape the Belle Mead facility. I had entered the valley of darkness. It was fast and frightening, and a full bottle of my medication sat right on the night-stand table. I opened it and started consuming them one by one—and then took a handful. I took the entire bottle, and not long after the room started to spin. The summer of 1978 nightmare had eclipsed into 1986, with a couple of teasers to horrify it, and now I was spinning like a top.

I remained standing for several minutes, but suddenly I began to fall. I remember collapsing, and as I fell, I saw a red blinking light on the phone. As I crashed, my left hand pulled the receiver off the phone.

When I awoke, I was in a cage: a room, about a ten-foot square, with a door at the end. That is the door I attacked over and over again, as described in Chapter 17. Above is how I got there. I was spared the valley of death; the fight was still ahead.

Don't give up. There's a rainbow at the end of this story I hope you will take a piece of.

There is nothing wrong, but everything right with hope!

CHAPTER 20

GLIMPSES INTO THE RAINBOW

I always loved the word spectrum. I gather because of the beautiful multicolor arc one sees upon the perfect angle, when light enters water droplets and bends, then reflects off the droplet's back side and bends again upon exiting. Yes, the observer actually has to be at exactly forty-two degrees opposite the light source to see the magnificent rainbow of the visible spectrum.

Sometimes it is that way with communication. Sometimes exact conditions need to be present, an audience void of outside concerns, but one filled with hope and willingness to take a roller-coaster ride, to envision another's point of view.

I didn't have those exact conditions in 2009 when I spoke with Dr. Rull. But that's okay, because when I met him in 2002, he was in disbelief over the list of medications I was on.

Please understand, today I have been symptom and medication free for the last eight years. No obsessions, no depressions, no delusions, no paranoia and no aberrations in thought—nothing but clarity of thought in some extremely stressful years for my wife and me, and our children.

Here is a list of medications I was prescribed and taking at age thirty-seven, not long after leaving medical school. While I do not recall if this was the exact list I was on when I met Dr. Rull, it is close.

1999 List of Medications

Lithium Salt of Carbonate: 1,800 mg/day

Antidepressant and Antiobsessive: 400 mg/day

Thyroid Replacement: Two pills each morning

Atypical Antipsychotic: Two twenty-five mg before bed

Antianxiety: One mg at bed

Beat Blocker :80-120 mg to prevent hand tremors

S.S.R.I: 100 mg

Antipsychotic: Five mg, if needed

I have to be honest my reader, after I typed out the eight medications above, tears rolled from my eyes. Dr. Rull took one look at this list after hearing my case history and shook his head in anger.

Seven years later and down to one medication, I walked into his office and told him my epiphany. In my excitement, I rambled about how I had reviewed my case history: events of burnout, psychosis, obsessions, depressions and more. I talked about all thirty-one years since the age of fifteen, all the medications, and the notion of the hypothesis that had come to me. I was sure about a baseline of neurochemistry, the concept of an adolescent predisposition, the idea of obsessional-thought stress keeping one locked in an obsessional loop, the power of the loop, the blasting of stress-driven cortisol against neurons, the need to break the cycle with medications, the adrenal-cortisol connection, the havoc the medications created on the balance of chemistry, generation of new symptoms and subsequent misdiagnosis, the medications driving the baseline up and down, and the need to consider personality type. *The Lindemann Theory* was in progress.

I was on fire, I kept saying, "What if? What if? and I am certain, certain, certain!"

And then I told him I wanted to be taken off the last medication I was on. I explained to him why. I told him I was certain: trust me, believe in me, but he could not.

I understood why he could not. I understood the risk it put him at professionally. Dr. Rull understood the neurochemistry I spoke of, but what I was asking him was to remove all pharmacological agents and let my brain come alive—alive in thought, creativity, confidence and strength. He understood my words on the power of food, long-chain essential fatty acids, and the power of exercise and challenge: intense, yet doable. I included the need of community to naturally retain balance, and the need to challenge the human body.

He was close to budging. I could sense his excitement, but societal pressures and genuine concern were against me. Thirty one years of illness and chaos were against me. And so, I left the office crushed and frustrated, and began my one-and-a-half-hour journey home. Ten minutes into the ride I said, "What if? And then I said 'yes'!" Yes, believe you me, it was time to hop on the roller coaster.

And so, over the next couple of months, I gently weaned myself off the last medication—yes against physician orders—but within a higher order's permission. I was following my own script of *InfinitE/ IQ*, while the last traces of medication left my body. The result was the rainbow.

And so, read on, my friends. I will present my theory and retro-spective analysis of my case history in detail. Read on, because I can no longer in good conscience let another person endure the pain I did and the confusion my team felt. I desire for all to see the glory this life beholds to the healthy and pure in spirit, mind and body. Read on, because a healthy recipe applies not just to the sick, but to the healthy. If you are sick in mind and/or body, read on. If you desire not to get sick and prevent, read on. If you seek peak performance, read on.

I figured it out. The word spectrum, and what it really means to me. It means a beautiful entity and phenomenon, made of many parts—some humans can see and some we cannot see, but the parts together in total: all of us can see—and it works.

Open your heart, and let your emotions paint the pages with words of passion, inspiration and knowledge!

Chapter 21

Oh, Canada or a Dangerous Drug Combination

With a celebratory birthday picnic in planning stages for my two girls, lawn and garden preparations were on the weekend list. The girls and I did manage to sneak into the house and catch an amazing special on the Costa Rican rain forest canopy.

The girls were transfixed by the magnificent colors displayed by the canopy hummingbirds, snakes, frogs, birds and flora. Darwinian evolution displayed its majesty in the vast spectral visage, well beyond the heptad of rainbow colors.

The girls were amazed a hummingbird visits 1,000 flowers a day for nectar, to maintain their ultra-high metabolic rate. Subsequently, we were introduced to one of the slowest metabolic rates on the planet, that of the three-toed sloth—a creature so slow in movement green algae have taken residence upon it. Then we discovered another mortgage-free critter living upon the sloth, the sloth moth.

All was well, until the narrator decided to describe the cycle of life and symbiotic relationship of the sloth and sloth moth in a bit more detail. You see, once per week, the sloth descends their tree to defecate (quite courteous, I thought). The moths hop off the fur and dine on this deposited product of waste. Eggs are laid and the moths hop back on the sloth on his next trip down: their cycle of life.

"Ew, disgusting!" my girls shouted, almost in unison.

They then asked almost simultaneously. "Did that moth just eat doo-doo, Daddy?"

I did my best, folks. I did my best as a parent, and I'm doing my best now. I will preface my summary of this visual by saying I love animals, and I love nature. I am a firm believer in the golden rule, and resist the temptation to judge others. Atop these declarations, I did my best to find a different adjective to describe this, well, state of being, living and existence:

What a shitty way to live!

No better time to segue back to 1983 and 1984.

As you recall, I had just attempted suicide after the experimental drug that performed admirably for thirteen months stopped working. My parents' research into alternate therapies, biofeedback, and orthomolecular and naturopathic techniques with two other doctors had proven fruitless. This all, of course, was precluded by a period of almost four years of unrelenting pain. The only break, of course, was the time spent in North Carolina.

With an entire bottle of drug consumed, the adverse effects had left me a human juggernaut, seeking escape from the cage room where I was placed. My last memory before awakening at the hospital in Belle Meade, New Jersey, was lying on the floor of that cage in another facility, physically and psychologically exhausted. I do not know how I came out of that savage state, or how long I remained in it.

Thirty-six hundred individuals were given the medication in those clinical trials. Research shows there were twelve overdoses. Two of those twelve died. The overdoses were up to 5,000 mg and plasma levels were up to 1,010 ng/ml. I swallowed hard when I read the two fatalities overdosed on amounts of 7,000 and 5.750 mg. I gulped because I took many, many, many pills, and would not be surprised if I were near the 5,000-mg mark.

Let's fight on.

My father had his own war going on when the overdose occurred. He was troubled the original facility I was taken to was unable to handle the situation. My comment: "Perhaps a zoo may have been a better destination. I presume we owed them a door as well?" We also were now without a doctor, as a horrific argument ensued, I was told later on.

Dr. Ham still oversaw my care, despite being at the Pennsylvania facility. When my father called her for advice after the suicide attempt, he was met with resistance. Apparently, Dr. Ham's sister had unexpectedly passed away. Dr. Ham's husband explained the impossibility of corresponding with Dr. Ham. Certainly, a strange position to take and say without compassion, as well I was told. My father understandably went ballistic. The relationship was severed. Dr. Hornalle at Carrier, the clinical trial coordinator, most likely had me transferred to his location.

Now a parent of two wonderful children, I cannot even imagine what my family went going through: a father's son alive, but in a horrible medical state, is in a heated argument with the husband of a reluctant physician. It closely rivals a son watching his father on death's doorstep, arguing at three a.m. about the visiting hospice after-care hours. My wife and mother needed you, people! I would have gone ballistic dad as well, and indeed did—no worries there!

And so, alive and recovered, I became a patient at the Belle Mead facility, taking residence on Edwards Hall. There I met a wonderful group of people, both patients and staff. The environment was invigorating, and at least the isolation was removed. It is this removal of isolation and the wonderful human environment that would lead to success in the many weeks ahead for me there at the hospital.

My new physician was Doctor Elm, simply a very nice man. He

was patient in case review, was without haste, and had a game plan as we immediately were met with some very large challenges. I no longer had access to the experimental drug, as I believe the overdose left me removed from the clinical trial. The possibility the drug failed because of lost sensitivity still pervaded in theory for me. So, if I were removed from the drug for a period, perhaps we could go to Canada and gain access to the drug. Remember, this was the drug that completely erased years of misery, thus the desire to travel.

As a reminder, this drug was not FDA approved in the United States. I could not get it prescribed in the normal manner. Was Canada a legal option? I was and am unaware at this time. Dr. Elm had a different idea, albeit a dangerous one. Perhaps a wise one for two reasons:

1) A suicide attempt does not indicate patient stability and a secure setting is desirable.

2) There was a low probability of success upon resuming the experimental drug.

Even if the theory of de-sensitization of serotonin receptors were valid, what length of time would be needed for sensitivity to return? Keep in mind, at the time I had no idea other pharmacologic options were available.

Dr. Elm wanted to pursue the usage of a drug combination. That combination consisted of an MAO inhibitor and another drug, which is a tricyclic antidepressant. While Dr. Elm explained the combination had some inherent risks. I was by no means aware of some of those risks I've discovered during research for this writing. Nor do I know if the below risks were documented when this combination was prescribed. Please note the description in italics, as taken today from drugs.com.

Using the MAO inhibitor I was prescribed, together with the tricy-

clic antidepressant I was prescribed, is not recommended. Combining these medications can increase the risk of a rare but serious condition called the serotonin syndrome, which may include symptoms such as confusion, hallucination, seizure, extreme changes in blood pressure, increased heart rate, fever, excessive sweating, shivering or shaking, blurred vision, muscle spasm or stiffness, tremor, incoordination, stomach cramps, nausea, vomiting and diarrhea. Severe cases may result in coma and even death. In general, you should wait at least fourteen days after stopping the MAO inhibitor I was prescribed before you start treatment with the tricyclic antidepressant I was prescribed. Conversely, if you have recently been on the tricyclic antidepressant I was prescribed and are now starting treatment with the MAO inhibitor I was prescribed, you should check with your doctor or pharmacist to see how long you should wait before it is safe for you to use the stated MAO inhibitor. As some medications can take a while to clear from your body, it is important to tell your doctor about all other medications you use, including vitamins and herbs. Do not stop using any medications without first talking to your doctor.

One component of the drug regimen prescribed to me is in a class of drugs known as monoamine oxidase inhibitors (MAOI), developed in the early 1950's. Hang in there, my reader, we're going to get into a little pharmacological action of the drugs, and I'm going to do my best to simplify these descriptions. Monoamine oxidase is an enzyme in the human body that exists in two forms: A and B. Type A works on serotonin and NE in brain tissue. Type B works on dopamine. Now, while it is felt the action of MAOIs on Type B is relatively inconsequential in the antidepressant and OCD-inhibiting effect, I may feel otherwise. I mention this because another drug, taken years later, was effective against a depression I fell into. It removed OCD symptoms, and had no serotonergic action. Rather, it inhibits the reuptake of dopamine and NE only.

Again, I come back to the same point. The neurochemistry behind OCD is complex. Three of the drugs (one of which was combination of two) during this thirty-one-year ordeal had both serotoninergic effects and NE effects and one had no serotoninergic effects, but both had NE and dopamine effects. The clear player in all four is NE, but it seems action on serotonin retains most credit for the therapeutic effects, SSRIs, on OCD symptoms. Perhaps the more astute take is to understand all of these neurotransmitters interact, have feedback loops and are interdependent. Again, perhaps a later writing will explore this, but nonetheless, we have a significant case drug record and effect. It is this very same record which I utilized to develop *The Lindemann Theory*, substitute *InfinitE/IQ* and remove side-effect-inducing medications for my ultimate cure.

In summary on this digression into drug action, it is imperative to understand the exact causation of the disorder of OCD. Like any disorder, the goal is to impair the illness with the most specificity and least side effects. But, as my theory will further extrapolate upon, the goal—once the brain-lock is broken—is to slowly remove the drug, and resume a healthy milieu with food control, long-chain fatty acids eicosopentaneoic acid (EPA) and docosahexaenoic acid (DHA) in fairly high doses, and a rigorous exercise regime, with a doctor's approval. *InfinitE/IQ* is comprised of mental and physical stimulation/exercise, community and clean fuel. It represents boundless energy and cognition. Nine plus years of symptom-free living, along with an explosion of creativity and analytical thinking, validates my theory. Five Hundred million years of evolution created a vulnerable—but magnificent—brain chemical balance that necessitates it!

We left off on Type A and B monoamine oxidase enzymes. We

see the following in regard to inhibiting Type A: within three days, inhibition of both the reuptake of serotonin and NE, leaving more in the neuronal synapse. But it is felt the two to three-week effect to be the most important. It is this same two to three-week effect that was pertinent with the experimental drug I took in the clinical trial. That effect being both a down-regulation of synaptic transmission mediated through noradrenergic alpha-1 and beta-adrenoceptors, and an up-regulation improvement of the transmission at serotonin synapses.

In summary, the MAOI I was prescribed allows increased firing of serotonin and NE from neurons over the three-week effect, while it leaves more available between neurons for both the three-day effect and the three-week effect. One might wonder if the MAOI, prescribed alone, would have been successful, or was considered. I have no answer for you, and only suggest it because of the overlap in action to the tricyclic antidepressant I was prescribed. I feel confident Dr. Elm had documentation evidencing OCD alone proved refractory to either the drug alone, and sought relief for me after a horrific suicide attempt.

Of great importance is that the MAOI alone, or in combination, presents certain risks. One must make dietary restrictions on food containing tyramine (beer, wine, certain cheeses, aged meats and more). The risk is a hypertensive crisis: an extremely high blood pressure event. The dangers of the combination of the MAOI and the tricyclic antidepressant I was prescribed have been stated above. The precipitation of mania and psychosis is rare with the MAOI, and no mention of this possibility was made at the time this drug was explored for me, although hypertensive crisis and food interactions were discussed. Again, in the serotonergic syndrome noted above, hallucinations were mentioned.

I would like to note at this time, the mentioned risk of this combination of drugs at the time of prescription was only in regard to the hypertensive crisis. There was no mention of the serotonin syndrome, as mentioned above. Please note: I experienced both burnouts and delusions, paranoia, hallucinations and psychotic breaks with both the tricyclic/MAOI combination and with taking the other drug mentioned above (with dopamine and NE action). With the clinical trial medication, I experienced burnout, but did not experience over-elevated mood symptoms such as delusions, hallucinations or euphoria.

With this said, I was only on the clinical trial medication for approximately thirteen months. For clarity, not once in my thirty one years of taking these mood-elevating drugs was it mentioned burnouts or over-elevation in mood might be attributable to the prescribed medications. Nor was the concept of reducing the dose discussed; this statement comes knowing these drugs have a therapeutic range. These statements concern me, as I summarize below.

Let me reiterate, these drugs are all designed to elevate neurotransmitters, and in turn mood. They are designed to leave more neurochemicals between brain-tissue neurons, and to increase release of neurochemicals from brain tissue. Also let me be clear, during this thirty-one-year ordeal, the concept of euphoria, mania, delusions and hallucinations are known to be the result of elevated neurotransmitter levels.

From the layman's aptitude, I believe anyone could define euphoria as feeling a little bit better than an elevated mood. From my own experience in having two psychotic breaks, both of which I am certain were the result of the medications prescribed, here is the progression of my experience: euphoria, leading to delusions and hallucinations, leading to a psychotic break. I will elaborate later, and define the term euphoria better, because it was actually a bit of an off feeling—as well as feeling too good. If I were asked did I enjoy this state, I could answer with certainty: no. I did not experience the effects of mania many have become familiar with, such as shopping and spending sprees and more. Again, any elevation in mood I experienced was in combination with an off feeling to it, so I actually would not even define it as a euphoric feeling. I did not enjoy it.

Let me continue and describe the tricyclic medication, part of this dangerous combination. The tricyclic antidepressant inhibits the reuptake pump for serotonin and adrenergic neurons. It is in the same class as experimental drug I took, having the same three-week long-term receptor changes. It does not directly stimulate the central nervous system. Understand, it has the same mechanism of clearance via cytochrome P450 2D6 as the experimental drug. It does have side effects of delusions and possible mania—again, overstimulation. I was unaware of this until research began for this book.

So thankfully, Dr. Elm had a plan with this drug combination. Canada became a moot point, and a new experiment was underway. The good news is I would be taking the drug combination in an environment that fostered its success; I would be among friends and have community. I understood the risks of a hypertensive crisis, and to avoid foods rich in tyramine. The why on the tyramine: as monoamine oxidase breaks this enzyme down, you leave too much in the body. This is dangerous because tyramine acts as a catecholamine-releasing agent that can cause dangerously high blood pressure.

We've gone from colorful frogs and snakes to green-hued excrement, door repairs and doctor snares, treatment options, drug combinations, lessons on drug interactions, pharmacodynamics (drug action) and pharmacokinetics (drug clearance), pitfalls in diagnosing, insights to my eventual recovery, removal of isolation and a return to community—and are left with hope. Hopefully, a new drug combination can break the brain-lock of OCD and lead us to final elucidation to treat others. And so, we can only say ...

There is nothing wrong, but everything right with hope!

CHAPTER 22

R, R and R, Community Family and Love

In Chapter 21, I advanced the concepts of pharmaceutical action on the human brain and opened up a discussion on the realities of side effects. Then it was noted that misinterpretation of side effects can lead to misdiagnosis, layering of medications and subsequent new sequela creation. While I have touched upon the expansiveness of the human brain and the attributes of conscious thought, language and more, it is of utmost important to understand the enlarged size of the neocortex specifically equates to a very social brain. Five million years of human evolution has, like it or not, made all of us interdependent.

Survival of our species necessitates cooperation. From a strictly biological sense, people need people, with conscious thought and the revelation of "me" also envelopes the need for "you". Narcissism, greed and apathy, if pursued, will destroy the human species. If the selfish three knock on your day, try to resist for the sake of the whole—mankind. We may be at a precipice in time and history where the selfish may no longer be tolerable. The former notation is by no means a philosophical take on life and living, but a reality in for the preservation of the species. Exhaustion and abuse of Earth's resources are but one simple but major example.

Thus, credence is given to the equation:

(Family + Friends) – Isolation = Quality Mental Health

I woke at three a.m. one morning to my wife Rosanne's pulsating abdomen. Her womb bounced up and down, and as we were but weeks from delivering our first child. I calmly freaked out. We threw on our clothes and hastened to the automobile—going away to the nearest E.R. was the plan. What was happening to our developing fetus? And so, it was with delight, laughter, joy, embarrassment and sleepy eyes, we learned young Rhaena had the hiccups. There is only one other time Rhaena in the womb acted in such a manner, and that was when my pregnant wife would listen to Susan Boyle sing "Hallelujah". At least then you could see feet kicking through her abdominal wall. Rosanne, Rhaena and I headed to the hospital emergency room that night. We were with family and friends, and we were without isolation.

When Rhaena was nine months old, the 4th R: Rochelle, was already developing in the watery home of Rosanne's uterus. At nine months, I would place Rhaena on the lawn and watch her sway left, then right, and scream "Timber!" as she fell. I only got to enjoy that for one month. At ten months as she walked, she shouted, "Mama!" one day with joy. The rest of her words would not follow for another two months.

With the birth of Rochelle, my reaction was no different, despite having gone through this one previous time. Tears strolled down my face as she emerged into the world. Rhaena had a baby sister, the ratio of women to men now three to one, and I knew my kingdom and throne had dwindled. The memories these two have given me, even at just five and six years of age, and my wife Rosanne—could last a lifetime. My favorite memory, of course, is a Christmas story; I believe December of 2015.

Following screams and crying from both children, the sounds took me to the foot of the stairs. I looked up and saw my two girls embracing each other, crying and literally shivering. Perplexed, I happened to look left into the family room and saw the eight-foot tree, with maybe two hundred ornaments sprawled across the carpet. Well, we got to decorate that tree all over again. No more tree climbing for any of us.

A king without a crown is a happy king, when surrounded by the likes of these 3Rs though. The Lindemann family came to feel the daily embrace of love. Our home, nestled in a small town in north-central New Jersey, allows all of us to discover neighbors, friends and community. The environment allows me to examine the sponge-like activity of my daughters' minds, and their thirst for knowledge and solutions. I watch them run and jump about the house and neighborhood with joy and boundless energy. They have a natural application of stimulation, one of my three components of *InfinitE/IQ*, and one which I call all of us to embrace again. The friends and family would help to define the second component of *InfinitE/IQ*: community.

It was a similar feeling of comradery and community I would feel upon admittance to the halls at the Belle Meade, New Jersey Mental Health Facility. And so, in regard to community one is only left to ponder, the rainforest conversation from sloth-moth children at the local playground.

"Hey Jimmy, where do ya live?"

"I live in shit!"

"Hey, man. Me too, me too. That's where I grew up!"

A friendship is born.

So, with the above message noted, our hearts opened up, let's head back in time—and see where this story takes us.

Open your heart, and let your emotions paint the pages with words of passion, inspiration and knowledge!

CHAPTER 23

THAT'S JUST THE WAY IT IS ...

This morning I entered my office feeling slightly groggy, and determined rapidly I was feeling the effects of a high-glycemic nighttime liquid snack: a mega-carbohydrate load, slid down unaccompanied by protein, and with enough saturated fat to leave my cell membranes stiff and uncommunicative. The liquid format was so high in surface area, and without fiber content, the pure glucose passage from stomach to bloodstream went unbridled. My body responded with pancreatic insulin release and rapidly dropping blood glucose levels. The accompanying lack of protein prevented my body's protective feedback mechanisms from achieving control.

My brain would endure a night of malnourishment. *Would my neuronal-insulating sheaths be restored effectively if I were unable to reach a restorative sleep?* High insulin initiates a biochemical nighttime nightmare, and while I slept delta-5 desaturase enzyme became activated, arachidonic acid increased, PGE1 controlling my neurotransmitters may have suffered in production and my body—now stressed—may have reached for cortisol production. If cortisol is produced, my hippocampal neurons might be destroyed.

And now you know why I only make the above mistake once in a while. Egg whites on an olive oil coated pan, blueberries, strawberries and honeydew melon slices cover my plate. Washed down with the ice-cold sprigged mint H2O, my counterattack to restore my biochemistry begins. Emersion of my cranial vault into the back-yard swimming pool is step two, while the music of Bruce Hornsby and The Range's *The Way It Is* completes this morning's restorative recipe. Certainly, while the decibel level this morning may have left some auditory hair cells trembling, I was ready to write Chapter 23.

That's just the way it is, some things will never change, rolled on for 4:57 minutes and left me longing to pen. And so, I ask the reader, what would indeed happen if all the world's humans felt this way? The take-home message I began in Chapter 22 was that man's only predator is himself. Apathy, accompanied by greed and narcissism, was labeled as a recipe for extinction.

Those 4:57 minutes define apathy at its foundation, and indeed acceptance of the very wrong—lunacy and idiocy, guarantees things will not change.

Recently I have heard some of the following from some of my associates, friends, business associates and family members. To be successful in today's world, you have to be a *chameleon*. Just be *positive, positive, positive, don't be political* (don't say what you believe), *keep it simple* and more along the same lines. In essence, don't take a stand, agree with everyone no matter what, smile away and let the next generation work it out. Can you imagine the impediment to progress if all embodied this belief system?

No, this is not a philosophical monologue, it is a common-sense tutorial on human progress and adaptation, applicable world-wide. On my home front, and a drift back in history, I am reminded of a group of fellows whose signatures stamp my own to the category of hieroglyphics. Adams, Jefferson, Franklin, Sherman and Livingston were courageous, in their beliefs, not orators of change, but instruments of change. Am I mistaken in my belief a leader leads with intelligent plans and action laden in optimism, and not with melodic words that satisfy all—and say nothing, and then do nothing?

On a personal note, I would love nothing more than to talk about trimming the hedges, and yet—would it get done? The reality of vibrating blades to the rattling of one's frame, and erupting pores of poison ivy two days post a wonderful hedge haircut, seems to be the needed action plan on my home front. Yes, I do fantasize about a hydrocarbon dowsing and ignition of greenery, but appropriate?

So, give me the courage, to label bullshit bullshit and speak from an intellectual heart. I will complete this book and commit to my goal; *the patient comes first.* If my words help prevent just one misdiagnosis, and eclipse one day of OCD pain, then I did something to bring change.

The above words come with purpose. Let me continue the story, as I walk the halls of the Belle Meade Health Facility in the summer of 1984. I am alive after a very dangerous suicide attempt. My body is streaming with a dangerous cocktail of an MAOI and a tricyclic antidepressant, my spirits alive with hope, and I am now a part of a community that has removed one demon of illness—isolation. The design of the medication regimen on my brain chemistry was simple: release more neurotransmitters and leave more hanging around in neuronal synapses.

The Belle Meade facility was a very well-organized and maintained mental health facility. The grounds were very well-maintained. It sported a swimming pool. The professional atrium was laden with green plants, and there were many therapeutic modalities. Aside from psychiatric and psychotherapy offerings, there was gymnasium activities and interactive hobbies, ranging from ceramics to wood working. A library, multi-choice cafeteria, pool room and café for visitors, help round out the facility. Of course, there was the lab and the Electroconvulsive Unit as well. The facility actually took on the term country club, a term I believe would have detrimental value. The only excess was one of care from most members of the community.

I would like to state unequivocally at this time, my belief that the environment itself, not just the medications I was taking, allowed me to once again recover fully during 1984. The removal of an isolating milieu and replacement with people and mental stimulus, leading to stress reductions, paved the way for the neurotransmitters to follow suit. On a molecular level, stress-induced cortisol hormone production is reduced, thereby decreasing hippocampal neuron destruction, and allowing increased firing at the same time with prescribed biologics. As a reminder to the reader, as an insight into how I developed my cure and as historical evidence, please remember what happened to me upon admittance to the University in North Carolina. I will simply say, I entered an exciting, invigorating environment and results were seen. We will see another event when I enter medical school some years later: another key piece of evidence.

The above is important to me, because when the 1990s came and insurance companies would no longer fund this type of environment, I feel mental healthcare took a step backward. Mental health patients need to be treated optimally and returned to society as rapidly as possible. This will reduce long-term health costs. Minimal treatment will exceed healthcare costs, and may indeed lead to life-threatening events and devastation to families and communities. Can I substantiate this with data? No, I cannot at this time. This type of study possesses so many variables I am not sure it is possible. I am offering a suggestion above, one which I believe to be substantial and life-saving. Perhaps the news in today's media will enhance my point?

The halls of not just Edwards Hall, but the other halls at the health facility, were filled with wonderful people from all walks of life and occupations. There was an adult hall, a drug addiction unit, an eating disorder unit, an adolescent unit, an elderly unit and others. The range of disorders covered bipolar disorder, dementia, phobias, anorexia, bulimia, schizophrenia, autism, depression, anxiety, OCD, drug addiction and combinations thereof. All of the patients were very normal people, taken from the abyss of loneliness and despair, and all embracing the chance to heal. All of us, very familiar with the 1975 movie *One Flew Over the Cuckoo's Nest*, were very quick to quip about the popular electronic chain's jingle and tag line, "At Crazy Eddie's *"His Prices are Ins-a-a-a-ane!."* I'm sure none of us ever expected to be at a mental health hospital. I'm sure none of us wanted to come back either.

Safe and nurturing, the hospital left me with friends as well. The MAOI and tricyclic antidepressant combination posed no immediate problems, though I could not achieve orgasm and ejaculation, as with the experimental drug. I watched my diet in avoidance of tyramine, and a couple of weeks went by without any changes in blood pressure: monitoring a potential hypertensive crisis was essential. I became a regular in the craft rooms, and did my best to remain optimistic, despite the still-ravaging obsessions.

And then, four to five weeks into the drug regiment, again I would see and feel magic. The MAOI/tricyclic combination once again lifted the obsessions 100%, mental health and clarity of thought restored. I had four to six weeks in North Carolina, I had thirteen months with the experimental drug, and once again I saw hope with an effective, albeit dangerous, recipe.

The summer of 1984 looked bright. My parents, for the last couple of years, worked on the construction of a summer home at beautiful Lake Wallenpaupack in Pennsylvania, and the summer of 1984 marked its completion. Returning to my New Jersey university for the fall of 1984 would not happen. I still needed to remain at the hospital for observation because of the delicacy of the drug combination. And so, I did. I began to run outside the facility grounds, and hit wood working to create a Lake Wallenpaupack sign for the Lindemann family. It was good to be alive. I also made a friend who would head a lifeguard team at a bath and tennis club in Palm Beach, Florida. He invited me to join the team, and I excitedly said yes.

I thanked and hugged many people when I was released from the hospital. Just six to eight weeks earlier I had overdosed, and was close to another dimension and a final, Earthly good-bye. My immediate plans upon departure were to live at the new lake house, where I took it upon myself to landscape the property. I went at it hard for about two weeks; the place looked great, and then it happened.

I had just finished the landscaping project, a few miscellaneous tasks remaining, when I awoke one morning, headed out with tools and felt it. It was the same feeling of burnout I had with the experimental drug after I had painted the family home. It was feeling of beyond exhaustion, and sort of a repulsion to walk the property and work on it. No connection was made to the drug combination for causation, which I would later do in 2009. I thought one day of rest would suffice.

I awoke the next morning, again a void of energy; it was as if it was siphoned off. It would be about two to three weeks before I returned to myself. It was not gradual return of energy either. Just as rapidly as the burnout arrived, it would leave. I awoke one morning, and I felt myself again. No medical explanation was given, nor attention given to the efficacy and mechanisms of the drug combination as being causative. I resumed my summer enjoyment of the beauty of the lake, and prepared for a new adventure in Palm Beach.

Lifeguarding on the shores of Palm Beach was exciting. It was to be a six or seven-month stint during the most incredible weather in Florida, October through May. I would share a room in the main facility, enjoy baked grouper for breakfast and lunch, lifeguard until five p.m. and whisked off on my bike to weight train in West Palm Beach at night. I had the pleasure of meeting some great people. I was able to make one ocean rescue of a small boy, and slept through my first hurricane. And, of course, I still am in disbelief at my answer to one of the owners of the Budweiser brand.

"Hey, Robert, would you like to train and sail our yacht around the world?" And get paid?

Can you believe, I told him I had to return to the university to study in the fall of 1985. Free world travel versus book-brain immersion; I believe that was the question. White pasty skin versus tan oiled bodies, book binders versus cleavage, desk isolation versus world exploration? Point made?

One month into the job, I walked up to one of the staff waiters. I felt confused and sleepy, maybe delusional. I remember waking up in an off-the-pool cabana bed. In retrospect, I believe I had my first indication of the described serotonin syndrome. The described burnouts were another side effect of the drug combination. I would go on to have three or four smaller burnouts while in Palm Beach. And then, when I left Palm Beach heading back to New Jersey, I stopped off at Disney World, and suffered another burnout that ruined my vacation.

Palm Beach was a wonderful experience, the side events of burnout and delusion went unexplained. Lifeguarding in Florida led me to a lifeguarding job at a resort on Lake Wallenpaupack, and there—at the lake house—I would live during the spring and summer of 1985.

I had one year completed at the state university. My health was restored, except for some unexplained events of burnout and one strange case of delusions and passing out. With life returned, some confidence returned. Maybe not just academics but baseball could fill the fall semester of 1985 at my New Jersey university?

Was the agony of leaving the baseball diamond in North Carolina gone as well? In 1981, my North Carolina coach sat down with me and said a prayer, when I explained my need to leave that wondrous town. I will always remember that. If nothing else, he left me with …

There is nothing wrong, but everything right with hope!

CHAPTER 24

LET IT GO?

The varsity baseball coach bought out a beast of a pitching machine to the auditorium of Franklin High School in March of 1979. Frigid temperatures and frosted baseball diamonds left about twenty-five varsity baseball prospects facing one of the noisiest, ugliest, rustiest and heaviest throwers most had ever seen. It had one speed, and the ninety-five-mph tennis balls being thrown down the right-hand side of the gym were so daunting, most facing it simply chuckled and found air in their swings.

I was sixteen now, a sophomore at school, and already about eight months into suffering from the obsessions that began in July of 1978. My turn came. I looked out at the cranking beast, and annihilated twenty straight balls right back at it. Indeed, those tennis balls were flying and moving, but as fast as they came in, the elastic rebound was just as great.

Blessed with athletic ability, and fast eyes and hands, I went on to play varsity as a sophomore, junior and senior, and was chosen as the MVP three seasons in succession. Other athletic accolades would follow: athlete of the year as a senior. Heavily recruited by a prestigious Ivy League school, I landed my heels in North Carolina.

There would always be a desire to return to the rock, and the fall of 1985 seemed to welcome a chance. Obviously a rough run since July of 1978, highlights to include:

1) Almost four straight years of nonstop OCD: a reprieve of four to six weeks while in North Carolina.

2) An experimental drug success lasting thirteen months, and a successful academic year.

3) A suicide attempt, post OCD-return and months of depression, and treatment options exploration.

4) A new drug combination, potentially offering success. Burnouts and delusions noted, but not linked at the time to the drugs.

An eye exam before baseball tryouts in the fall of 1985 seemed prudent. I was aware I was having trouble seeing when I was playing night games in North Carolina. The eye exam left me with a written prescription, and the glasses arrived near the day of tryouts. I never put them on until that tryout. My ophthalmologist was elated at my restored mental health and baseball plans; as you recall the obsessions were somehow triggered by a routine eye exam, years earlier with him. About two weeks before tryouts at the university, I heard a story over the radio concerning a student losing eligibility by switching from one school to another. I had played one full game in full uniform in North Carolina, so I made a quick stop over at the university field house and confirmed with the coach this was of no concern in regards to eligibility.

And so, I stepped onto the university's baseball field that first day of tryouts, unknowing the manufacturer of the glasses had inserted the wrong set of lenses. So bad was the mistake, it was lucky I was not killed on the field, yet I would not realize the glasses were in error until the next day. I had never worn glasses, and simply thought you threw them on and away you go, typically the case with this said.

At shortstop, I began to field balls, throw and perform double plays. I could not catch the ball or see first base to reach with accuracy. Again, I had no clue as to what was occurring. The coach decided to find a reason to create a scene from home plate while hitting fungoes and began to harass me with screams of criticism. Intuition told me to let the man rant, I waited until he stopped, then turned and returned to the shortstop hole. I took three steps, and he came after me again. I played "his game", returned and listened again to his chastising until he stopped. I then again returned to the hole, and he did it all over again. Yes, I pretty much broke down, and headed off the field. The coach was very successful in getting me off that baseball diamond, but he wasn't done yet.

We were to take batting practice next, and warm-up swings to occur on a side-netted baseball cage. Keep in mind, you have about twenty-five people on this field, I have met this man for a total of two minutes two weeks earlier, and have no idea what his intentions nor problems were. I go to take my warm-up swings and notice the home plate and the surrounding footing is sitting in about six inches of sand. I immediately recognized swinging in sand would only exhaust my legs, so I chose to forgo the practice swings, saving my legs for the fifteen balls to come on the field. Those pitches would be my only redemption after the infield fiasco and humiliation.

Now this is crazy. So here we are, with maybe twenty-five people on the field, and this coach runs over to the netted area, way out of his way, and begins to harass me about not taking practice swings. I gently explained the sand depth, the expenditure of leg energy and my need to do well on the swings on the field as reasons for me by-passing the practice swings. He agreed and told me I would have trouble making the team. I said internally, *Gee, really, I couldn't catch a baseball on the field.* I proceeded to take my swings, and at the end of the fifteen you were to run the bases. I missed fourteen straight balls, got jammed on the last and hit it over the left field wall. He collapsed the field on me as I ran the bases, his final attempt at humiliating me.

Well, Coach, you were successful. I went home, packed my bags and headed to live up at Lake Wallenpaupack. I had lived a living hell since 1978. I was trying to get my life back to some order, and wouldn't you know it, I had to meet this guy. I would miss the fall of 1985 and spring of 1986 semesters at the university, as I withdrew from classes. I would not really pick up a baseball until some twenty years later. Yes, the game I loved so much would leave me for two decades. Perhaps fortuitous, as when I came back to the game, I taught myself all over again how to hit and throw. And I love to teach others, and feel I am one of the best at it.

And so, you have to tip your hat to this teacher of young men. The coach in North Carolina said a prayer for me, and this coach drove me to prayer. Nothing more needs to be said. You know I am tempted, but I will do my best to let the above words delegate a message. That is all I can do.

Open your heart, and let your emotions paint the pages with words of passion, inspiration and knowledge!

CHAPTER 25

THE MOUNTAINS AND A WINDOW

Last night I kissed my three girls good night on the forehead, and headed into the garage to bench press super-set style for twenty minutes. The exercise was done in a manner where heart rate was maintained for aerobic development, and with an intensity that would activate dormant stem cells and initiate their release. Brain-derived neurotropic factor (BDNF) production would be increased, as well as endorphins. A steady flow of glucose would reach my brain all night. Actin and myosin filaments were now ready to replicate and new muscle units were to follow, then angiogenesis and new neural connections in suit.

I entered the kitchen and dipped some grilled chicken in guacamole, and tossed some seedless red grapes and honeydew chunks upon my plate, all chased with liquid EPA and DHA, and icy H2O with a flotsam of orange, lemon and lime to follow. I ascended the staircase, lifted my eyebrows and watched any remaining stress fade ceiling—then skyward. A restorative sleep would follow.

The above description is a general outline of a component of *The Lindemann Theory*, a philosophy and lifestyle that might allow thousands of OCD, and other patients, to find peace, health and live medication free.

As much as Chapter 24 has tempted me to rationalize the addition to mental health facilities of a JAFA unit, you and I must further continue to explore the evidence to support my suppositions and establish new treatment protocols. At bear minimum, let's raise awareness and begin questioning.

Let us continue as I venture into the woods in 1985 and 1986, return to lifeguarding at a resort overlooking Lake Wallenpaupack and keep my eyes and hands moving with a bit of mixology at the Montage Ski Resort. The resort owner welcomed me back with open arms to preside over the pool. When the pool season was over, offered a course in bartending in Scranton, Pennsylvania that led me to a job at Montage Mountain.

Skiing on the mountain, a Grand Marnier Lodge festival, log-splitting and cabin fires led me into the spring. I would meet a physician in Scranton, a wonderful woman, who first prescribed lithium to treat my burnouts. While she is no longer with us, it does pain me to say this prescription would go on to perpetuate a misdiagnoses and errant medication additions throughout the next twenty-five years. Of course, the lithium would eventually cause nephrogenic diabetes insipidus. Most importantly, the origin of the burnouts, delusions, paranoia and psychotic breaks that would interrupt my life up until nine years ago were never examined. Bandages led to more bandages—and more patches to follow. Like bad computer code, a simple fix gets clouded and exacerbated to an impossible complexity.

With the winter season over, I would move back to New Jersey, find another bartending job, take summer classes at my New Jersey university and gear up for a full semester in the fall of 1986. And yes, it would happen again. I would score a 95% on my first organic chemistry test, and out of the blue, a six week burnout would cause withdrawal of classes from school. Perplexed and exhausted, I hung in there and found a window of hope.

And so, from the spring of 1987 to the summer of 1989, I would complete two degrees at Rutgers, one in biology and one in psychology. I would do so with high academic standing, and while taking some very advanced classes. I did not bartend on weekends during this period, the removal of stress is another piece of evidence I would use to navigate my cure. I had a nice run without burnouts and thought it was over; a reasonable assumption with no knowledge of causation yet.

With resume in hand, I went to my first job interview at a major pharmaceutical company, and it was there I first found interest in a career in medicine. The job I was interviewing for involved running assays for a group of PhDs. The first gentleman looked at my coursework and asked would I not get bored at this job. He brought up the possibility of, "Rob, why don't you go to medical school?"

Perplexed, I walked and chatted with the second PhD. He studied my transcripts and said, "Rob, why don't you just go to medical school?"

Further bewildered, I approached the third PhD, and he put his arm on my shoulder and bought me to the corner of the lab in a covert manner, as I studied the cup of coffee shaking in his other hand.

"Robert, listen, I need your opinion on something. My son wants to borrow money from me to start his own business. Rob, what do you think I should do?"

His hands trembled, and he stammered a bit.

So, I asked if he had any faith in his son and faith in his business plan. Was the son responsible? I ran the gamut of questions for him. His head shook left to right, with negatives, and then he gave one final positive nod, as he reached a conclusion. He never asked me any questions about the job. I spent most of the conversation concerned the coffee was going to spill as he trembled. Obviously I thought, was this how interviews in America normally go?

And so, I walked into the parking lot and I thought, I enjoy helping people, have compassion and empathy, and love the science of the human body—and it was decided. I was proud of completing my studies and thought the burnouts were behind me. I began my MCAT (Medical Aptitude Testing Studies), took the test and began the application process for medical school.

I loved the decision. Medical School had not occurred to me as a career option. I wished those gentlemen well. If I carried the MD degree, I would recommend decaffeinated coffee and a vacation to my last interviewer. I anticipated a bad week for him, and his son …

There is nothing wrong, but everything right with hope!

CHAPTER 26

OPPOSITE ENDS OF THE SPECTRUM

Rhaena and Rochelle were so excited this morning as we ran the halls—slightly late—of Rochelle's pre-school and summer camp facility in search of the gardening class on the second floor. With our destination found and Rochelle now a participant, Rhaena sought competition with her dad upon exiting: she to take the elevator and me the stairs one flight down—to see who would be the victor. I sprinted hard, took a knee outside the stainless elevator door and stuck my tongue out. When the door opened, she giggled and laughed uncontrollably, took two steps forward, and gave me a huge hug. It felt so good.

I held her at arm's length and smiled. She was full of beauty and joy, suggesting we be late more often, as the rush still left her giggling. The summer of 2017 left her natural olive-hued skin with an even darkened tan, UV radiation stimulating her melanocytes to release even more melanin for protection. Fortunately, her mother's Guyanese blood blessed her with a few more melanocytes than my Norwegian and German complexion, although this summer even I am sporting a tan. Her mother also blessed Rhaena and Rochelle with her natural beauty, inside and out as well.

I told Rhaena why the summer of 2017 was important for me. I whispered in her ear, the summer of 2017 would set her daddy free.

She smiled again, and nodded with partial understanding. I dropped Rhaena off next. With the thoughts of her excitement about the morning and melanocytes driving a tan in my mind, it was time to expand on the core of the hypothesis I developed eight years ago: my cure for OCD. No, the word cure has no quotes around it, not "cure", but cure. Hang with me, reader, as I hope to write with clarity when explaining *The Lindemann Theory*.

With melanocytes in mind, I was reminded of how there is an intermediate lobe of the pituitary gland in some lower animals, sitting between the anterior and posterior lobes. Man also has a pituitary gland in his brain with both an anterior and posterior lobe. And so, in these animals, the hypothalamus is stimulated by the sun, which in turn activates MSH (Melanocyte-Stimulating Hormone), which in turn activates melatonin to release melanin.

Next time you're in the arctic in the summer and you wonder why your favorite animal's winter white coat has now become darkened, you will know why. This would be an environmental affect that causes a physiological change in an animal, as with man and UV light's activation of melanocytes. You, as the reader, were also just exposed to a cascade of events, if you will:

Sun ➤ Hypothalamus ➤ Pituitary ➤ MSH ➤ Melatonin ➤ Melanin ➤ Darker Skin

If you do not have a broad biological background, I am simply engaging in a slow tutorial at the moment—hang in there.

MSH is in humans as well, along with adrenocorticotropic hormone secretion (ACTH), beta-lipotropin and beta-endorphin that is released from the anterior pituitary, when it is activated by cortisol-releasing factor (CRF). This factor comes from the hypothalamus.

ACTH, when released by the anterior pituitary, goes on to activate cortisol from the adrenal cortex of the adrenal gland. In turn, cortisol can feed back and inhibit either the anterior pituitary or the hypothalamus, but this protective mechanism can be overridden by stress stimuli. In other words, the human being can push themselves, and in effect, bypass this protective feedback loop.

It is in this control system where I developed my ideas concerning burnout, and the notion that the stress and pain of OCD obsessions can retain an individual in a locked brain, with an endless loop of pain and stress. Remember, cortisol directly destroys neurons within the hippocampus. Also remember, the medications I was taking were designed to dump and leave, and fire more of one or more of the following neurotransmitters, serotonin, NE and dopamine.

Remember, the dangerous MAOI/tricyclic combination I was taking during university, admission to medical school and eventual entrance to medical school, were designed to double up on the effect of increased neurotransmitter storage (prevent break down) and increased firing (release). In final for this discussion, remember when I entered North Carolina, there was a complete cessation of obsessions via a natural neurotransmitter boost from an environmental effect: a regular life effect.

So, there was purpose in describing my two daughters joy and laughter this morning. Their exuberance was like the finale of a fireworks display: picture the dispersal of explosions, as your brain's 100 billion neurons fire away. Neuron synapses flood with euphoric chemicals; action potentials fly down axons, sodium and potassium channels fly open and shut; voltages changing lightning fast; and neuronal dendrites read the excitement in the air—responding with "fire more".

No wonder my daughter smiles, laughs and says, "Daddy, let's be late tomorrow again." No wonder I reach out and embrace her warmth and love, and exclaim I need to set myself free this year—this summer.

The very essence of my hypothesis, and one which is possibly void in thought for the physician, therapist, scientist or layman never to have had the "privilege" of nonstop obsessions—is that the patient views these thoughts as real. To others, the thoughts are viewed as ridiculous, even approaching humorous, notions. For the patient, the obsession creates stress, anxiety and pain, and a lot of it.

As I mentioned, one of my favorite television shows involved the interaction of Jack Klugman and Tony Randall in the series *The Odd Couple*. Yet as entertaining and comedic were the skits, the unintended message regarding the disorder of OCD could be tragically misleading. Felix, if afflicted with OCD, would be in despair and pain, and riddled with anxiety: not "Happy and peppy and bursting with love!" By all means, let's leave some room for the human (not OCD) who happens to be a "tad overly neat or anal ". This, of course, is a preference—and not a clinical disorder.

It is time to put this all together. We have the environment, consisting of life and life situations, we have biochemistry and physiology, and then we have medication biochemistry or pharmacology.

Let's start with an OCD patient, who has driven one mile from his home, and then wonders if he may have left the gas stove knob on and unlit, sending carbon monoxide through his home. He tells himself, "I know I turned it off". This thought leads him two miles down the road. He finally succumbs to the idea, goes back home and checks to make sure all is well. All is well, and he starts down the road again. He is three miles down the road, the idea of a gas leak having never left. The obsession builds, and he is forced to turn around again, despite being ten miles away from home this time. The whole scenario goes on for another four hours, leaving the afflicted individual writhing in agony, mentally stressed, humiliated, frustrated, riddled with anxiety, sweaty, confused, fearful and distraught. His only savior is a new concern: the banana peel he threw in woods earlier might kill someone via slippage.

On the cellular and body level, the stress activates almost instantaneously with an increase in ACTH. This is known to be caused by stress-induced activation of the limbic system, most notably the regions of the amygdala and hippocampus. They, in turn, signal the hypothalamus. Understand, it is known human or mental stress can, within minutes, activate ACTH. Then the adrenal cortex releases increased cortisol almost twenty-fold in amount. Understand, as well, cortisol is an extremely powerful hormone, and known to cause neuron brain cell destruction in the hippocampus, a region of importance in lost serotonin production and OCD causation. Does the cortisol destroy neurons elsewhere? Another medication I would take years later in the story, also sequestered OCD, yet acted on dopaminergic and NE hormones.

So, we have a human, already embroiled in obsessive thoughts because of sub-baseline neurotransmitter levels. The very thoughts are creating stress and cortisol, damaging the very neurons needed for recovery. In effect, we have a devastating, disastrous, self-contained destructive loop. No wonder the thoughts don't stop. Remember, we discussed cortisol can feed back and stop ACTH production, but the stress can override this mechanism—and does. Anti-anxiety medications don't help; why would they? The thoughts create the anxiety: to stop the anxiety, you need to stop the thoughts. Anti-anxiety medications are not intended to stop obsessions.

The idea of using natural means to restore the balance is not a bad one, but the self-destructive nature of the loop most likely precludes this means from working; balance can't keep up with destruction. And so, we see the need for either direct pharmacologic intervention, and I have pondered whether alternate ECT methods might be effective? Psychotherapy makes little sense, outside of nurturing, because the origin in my case was biologic and not created by aberrant ideologies, at least for me. The other mentioned concern was, of course, the pain level and chance of suicidal ideation, and desire to rapidly remedy the OCD patient.

And so, in 2009, I recognized the causation at the molecular level. I understood the brain-lock loop, the need for pharmacologic help, the *danger* of psychotherapy in remedying my OCD, my thirty-one year case history, and the reasons for failure of natural means in breaking the lock. I discovered the latter to be the final piece of the puzzle when achieving an ultimate cure.

No better time than to jump directly into what I have previously described as side effects and sequelae, resulting from the medications I was taking to break the brain-lock. Those side effects consisted of burnout periods (during physical and/or mental work), paranoia, and euphoria, delusions, hallucination and psychotic breaks. This represents a second component of my theory. The first is breaking the brain-lock, the second: the goal to restore balance without medications as they cause side effects. The final component is the means to restore a natural brain-chemical balance.

For the moment, we will just explore the burnouts and causation. We will then head back into my story, which will in turn provide a natural gateway to the creation of euphoria, delusions, hallucination and psychotic breaks in my clinical history. The story will also take the reader to me having endured four major bouts with depression. I do not attribute the depressions to the medications I was taking, but rather view them as creations of my environment and life situations. With this said, that environment existed because the side effects of the medications led to it. Make no mistake though, depression—once begun—involves altered neurochemistry, and for others the very origin may be in altered neurochemistry.

Hang with me reader, we are almost detail-free. What are the medications designed to do? They are designed to boost brain chemistry. Caffeine is a stimulant, and many of us have experienced the burnout effect of caffeine—albeit a day or two in longevity for most. What would happen if more powerful exogenous chemical were taken? Could they override the cortisol feedback loop we have already described?

That was my thought eight years ago, and the fact I have been symptom and burnout-free since then validates it. If the medications allow one to work even a little longer and harder than normal, would not the brain-adrenal-cortisol loop become overworked, and eventually become exhausted? Again, we know the cortisol feedback loop can be overridden. If the human so chooses, he can continue to put demands on ACTH, adenyl cyclase and cyclic AMP until they are over-activated and used up when calling for more cortisol from the adrenal gland. We overuse the control systems, and the result is a total body shut down: for me three to eight weeks of burnout, with devastating life effects and expense. Then, of course, depression drawn in.

The mere fact our hormone systems have been 500 million years in development, and modern man has been five million years in development, suggests a system of immense complexity and balance, as noted previously. The concept of reducing complexity, and feeding the natural system its base components seemed prudent, and has proven prudent.

And so, I have delineated one end of the spectrum for you, the burnout and adrenal exhaustion of my clinical history. It is time to return to applying to medical school, and my acceptance to medical school. More importantly, it is time for the reader to formulate their own hypothesis. I will be attending medical school under the following neurotransmitter conditions.

1) An Environmental Boost – Excitement and Adventure (remember the North Carolina Phenomenon)

2) MAOI Medication – A Neurotransmitter Upper

3) Tricyclic Medication – Another Neurotransmitter Upper (Both Together Can Cause Serotonin Syndrome)

4) My Type A Personality, Also a Neurotransmitter Upper

It is not just a triple whammy; we've got a quadruple whammy brewing. Let me know your thoughts on the spectrum. Which end do you think I'll be at when I begin my first year of medical school? We will get there, but first in Chapter 27, I would like to describe the process of my acceptance to medical school.

Above was bit of a roller coaster, the description necessitated by my desire for others to avoid it. The brain-adrenal-cortisol axis is a powerful one, one which we must respect. This control system normally requires no fertilizer. Nourishing the balance shall be our goal.

Open your heart, and let your emotions paint the pages with words of passion, inspiration and knowledge!

Chapter 27

Interviews of Polarity, Claws of Steel and Flying into the Cuckoo's Nest

This morning I drank from a refrigerated jug of water, chilling overnight as the flavors of soaking cucumber, lime and fresh-sprigged mint erupted into my thirst-quenched palate. I loaded my daughter's backpack with plastic bottles of water with hesitation, with reluctance because of a reading I took the day prior.

Yesterday afternoon, the girls and I enjoyed a New Jersey nature preserve, where we picnicked, face-painted, taste-tested Jersey peaches, and trolley-toured lakes, waterfalls and sculptures. I spotted an Eastern Goldfinch, New Jersey's state bird, darting amongst a line of sycamores—this left us complete. Is there anything better than a New Jersey white peach?

While the girls refreshed at the visitor center, I wandered into a nature education room, and came across some facts on plastic water bottles. Those facts referred to the forty billion plastic bottles produced in the U.S. per annum, the millions of tons of greenhouse gases released upon plastic manufacturing and the 700 years to begin composting if one does not reach recycling.

So, I asked, "What are we doing? Seven-plus billion people on this rotating sphere; what are we doing?"

I gladly took my mother to her annual physical this morning. The dietary recommendations I made to her fifteen years ago, and her morning consumption of some long-chain fatty acids seemed to have had health and anti-aging benefits as she strolled up the office steps with fluidity. Soon to be ninety-two years old, her blood chemistry panel is usually better than the rest of us. Her afternoon routine of a half-hour bike ride and a half hour on the treadmill is never missed. It drives my wife crazy with guilt.

In the waiting room, I jotted down notes for this afternoon's penning, while glancing at a naturopathic television station mounted high and cornered. The lead actor, an apparent advocate of eggs, explained the cholesterol in eggs is not the problem, but rather the foods eggs are paired with at breakfast. With sincerity, I estimate the average American loses 25% or more of daily productivity because of what they nourish their bodies with, and neglect in exercise. While I will hold off on expanding, allow me to settle my angst created by the egg advertisement.

The truth: egg yolks contain arachidonic acid (AA), which is a precursor to the formation of unwanted eicosanoids, a group of very powerful proto-hormones that sit at the foundation of the human body's biochemical network. AA is also found in organ meats and fatty cuts of meat, folks. AA is an undesired chemical, a really bad "egg". One fundamental goal of food balance is to direct dihomo-gamma-linolenic acid (DGLA) towards good proto-hormones, and away from activating an enzyme called delta-5 desaturase, which turns DGLA into AA, and then to undesirable proto-hormones. The last thing you want to do is directly ingest AA, since our main goal is preventing its formation.

So, what are we doing? As part of *InfinitE/IQ*, there will be a call for clean fuel.

I can only conclude one of two things, when I view this type of public message.

A) The station is uninformed.

B) The station is paid to be uninformed.

I lost thirty-one years, and no longer want you or my kids to be uninformed. I can't make those years up. I accept they are gone, but I can do my best to create longer ones and conserve DNA.

As you can see, life (reflections, family and "rotten egg" commercials) has derailed my immediate penning from Chapter 26 right into Chapter 27, but perhaps this is best. I've expanded on the idea that nourishing our biochemistry correctly, love and community, and challenging our wits and bodies will provide enjoyment and longevity. Yes, the sad note on integrity of information should be keenly noted, holistic propaganda to be noted as "Holes in Holism" and truth are even at odds.

The end of Chapter 26 left the reader with a bit of a puzzle, a question asked to predict a quadruple whammy as I head off to medical school. An environmental boost, with an MAOI and tricyclic boost with a topper of Type A personality behind it, is predictive of what? One last riddle before we dive right in.

What am I?

Transient yet memorable

Rarely seen, but always there

Low chance for one, High for many

When done, one of many remains

When 27 is completed, the what will be deleted.

Before we head off to medical school, let me first take you on a tour of the interviews that preceded my acceptance. With collegiate transcripts in hand, community and hospital volunteering, and medical college admission tests successfully taken, the application process to medical school had begun. During this time, I worked both at the family business and a few evenings of mixology, which actually turned into some pretty brutal exercise routines.

Certainly, the dean of students from an Illinois medical school made an impression on me. I never had a more comfortable interview in my life. The location of the school was around the suburbs of Chicago, but an intermediary location was selected for the interview. I enjoyed sharing my New Jersey education, and my excitement about this new career possibility. The dean was a true gentleman, and simply felt a click and warmth about his aura. I was full of optimism, joy and energy.

That was one end of the spectrum. I had another interview that bordered on the bizarre and inexplicable, and definitely was at the other end of the spectrum. I arrived at the medical school campus, and was greeted by a receptionist. She walked me to another building, and she remarked in our conversation along the path I sounded confident. I explained I was excited. I wanted to share all of my science experience while at university in New Jersey. Some of my favorite courses were comparative morphology, neuro-psychopharmacology, exercise physiology, genetics and general physiology. We also performed some exciting laboratory work: examples included stereotactic surgery, tracheotomies and multiple species dissections. My coursework in both degrees, biology and psychology were dedicated to the human body, a great foundation for the field of medicine.

I was greeted by my interviewer and immediately given my seat, and the gentleman took his seat. I was seated to the left of a magnificent bookcase with dimensions of seven to eight feet in height, five feet in breadth and two feet in depth. The gentleman sat to the right of the bookcase. We both faced the interviewer's desk, his name plate reversed on the desk, so I might see. The gentleman was either a professor of psychology, PhD or a psychiatrist, MD or professor. I could not see the gentleman from where I was sitting, and he could not see me. We both stared at the wall behind his desk.

I do not recall a single question asked during this interview, nor do I recall a single answer given. What I remember was a very brief, cold and awkward meeting. It was, unquestionably, the most bizarre non-human to non-human interaction I've experienced—only paralleled by an unusual date I once had. By all means, I am no expert at dating. I do advise, though, waiting at least ten minutes before you tell your date you have the ability to see ghosts. I relayed the interview story once to one of my psychiatrists; he shook his head in knowing disgust. Yes, I too wonder if this represented an interview unlike other candidates received: the purpose, I cannot imagine – yet can.

I was overjoyed when I received the call from the dean of the Illinois medical school where I was accepted: classes to begin July 23, 1990. The nightclub I worked at on weekends took up a collection for my tuition, and we celebrated after a busy Saturday night. Family members were excited as well. I thirsted for the knowledge to help others. I longed to satisfy the Hippocratic Oath upon reaching the status of a practicing MD.

I swear to fulfill, to the best of my ability and judgment, this covenant ...

I will respect the hard-won scientific gains of those physicians in whose steps I walk, and gladly share such knowledge as is mine with those who are to follow.

I will apply, for the benefit of the sick, all measures which are required, avoiding those twin traps of overtreatment and therapeutic nihilism.

I will remember that there is art to medicine as well as science, and that warmth, sympathy and understanding may outweigh the surgeon's knife or the chemist's drug.

I will not be ashamed to say, "I know not," nor will I fail to call

in my colleagues when the skills of another are needed for a pa-
tient's recovery.
I will respect the privacy of my patients, for their problems are
not disclosed to me so the world may know. Most especially must
I tread with care in matters of life and death. Above all, I must
not play at God.
and more ...

With bags and my vehicle packed to the hilt, 80 West awaited. I
would cross Pennsylvania, Ohio and Indiana, followed by the sky-
scrapers of Chicago and into the 'burbs of North Chicago, where I
would land. The school was magnificent, and the Woodlands apartment complex next door would be my residence. Green Bay Road,
with an (847) area code—and the human body—would become my
life.

The opening curriculum was a blast: molecular cell biology, human genetics, clinical anatomy, embryology, medical ethics and
biostatistics. What ease today, to have these books in an electronic
format: not to mention 3-D virtual views and videos. I just lifted my
1,400-page medical school pathology book; it must weigh twenty
pounds. Those books used to rip up my forearm flexors and exten-
sors, and leave my fingers in a flexed rigor.

I made friends, furnished a small shared apartment, took in a kitten as a companion and hit the studies hard. All was going well, but
in retrospect there were some small indicators of a brewing storm.
On the trip out to Chicago, I noticed an unusual feeling during a stop
for a meal. The best I can do to describe it is a bit of an off-euphoric
feeling, with an inner intuition or perception, that all was not right. I
felt if such a state advanced further, I might sort of fall "off the shelf".
And with that intuition, there was also an element of fear, and with

that fear there was cognition the fear would facilitate the shelf fall—an entrance to psychosis.

As the reader, I would like you to reexamine that last sentence. It is my belief, it is this element of fear that drives individuals to have repeat anxiety attacks once they have had one. I say this never having had an anxiety attack, but close to it once. Certainly, it is also this element of fear that perpetuates the loss of control, once one obsession has occurred. And so, a lesson for the clinician and for the layman is to understand and recognize this fear, so it does not propagate lost control.

If you the reader cannot see this, it is OK and be glad. Most likely, you have never had a "mental event". Certainly, an analogy to the physical might suffice. Whereas one's fall off a motorcycle might be beneficial in making one more prepared for the next pothole, the fear of losing mental control has the opposite effect: exacerbation of the condition.

I would feel this off feeling repeatedly during my first one and a half months. I note this in retrospect. At the time I was unable to establish meaning or relevance to it. In Chapter 26, I described what I perceived to be precursors to a storm: two medications designed to boost mood, a natural high-life environment event of acceptance and attending medical school—and, of course, I noted the Type A personality as being contributory.

Of course, I plan on expanding later why I believe clinicians should take special note of Type A individuals and medications. The short course is a Type A individual who can drive themselves, coupled with medications that can pronounce this effect, can really boost mood. On the other end of the spectrum: the burnouts. A medication given to a Type A patient can drive them and curtail the protective feedback mechanisms of cortisol control, thereby facilitating burnouts. Certainly, I believe, a study associating personality type with side effects and sequelae of euphoria, hallucinations and burnouts from mood elevators might bear this out.

The described quadruple whammy: two drug highs + one natural high + one Type-A = four highs equates to a pressure cooker—and what might be percolating is the question.

Then it happened, and I had no chance to decipher the math problem. I do not believe there was a triggering factor, but rather a slow progression of brain chemical imbalance. Home alone one night after I had fixed a quick dinner, the euphoria seemed to make me even more flighty, and the kitten began to play a game of jumping on my bear-skinned back. The kitten repeated this as I felt delusional. That delusional and dizzy state drifted into a hallucinating state, where I felt I was under attack by this strange beast, my back being clawed with steel nails.

I knew I was in trouble. I felt wobbly in addition to flighty, the fear accelerating the rocky thrusters, and did my best to grab the phone and call a friend. My last recollection was to implore my friend to get to the apartment immediately, and possibly made mention of a need for an ambulance. It may be that I asked the friend to save the cat, who was in danger? Then I simply must have fallen of the shelf, and recall no more.

I was hospitalized. The rainbow was over and the riddle solved: a rainbow. I was devastated, as I had to withdraw from medical school on Sept 18, 1990 on a leave of absence. It was North Carolina all over again. It was my New Jersey university all over again. *How much could I take?* While I managed to finish biostatistics and medical ethics, all other coursework was again lost. Two months of hammering away, lost. A devastating drive back to New Jersey became the reality, and I went right back into isolation. It would be another year to wait, July 1991, before I could start medical school again.

That drive was brutal, maybe even more so than the trip back from North Carolina. At least with the drive back from Carolina, I had the anguish of the obsessions to replace the depressing thoughts of what just happened. Everything was going well, studies, academic life, great professors and the entire environment—and then the hammer was leveled, the window was shut, the environment was changed and a new riddle emerged.

The new riddle, of course, is where would the merry-go-round on the neurotransmitters go? Would the medications override and rule my life, the life only emerging because of the medications? Another circle, more pain and more confusion seemed imminent. I only wish someone figured out the problem, the solution that emerged to me nine years ago. And so, my reader, all was not over, but the struggle would eventually find me a rainbow at last. That is all I can do, is hope and there is …

There is nothing wrong, but everything right with hope!

CHAPTER 28

STOP AND THINK: TORTOISE AND THE HARE RE-VISITED

Riddle: *What is it?*

Chapter 27 bought anew, in 29, the riddle stews

While 28 delves to better sense

The what that's here, is revered

Can be up and down and all around

Defined by all, meanings vary

Icy cold or Fiery hot

Desirous to go, that is a not

Romanced as Lit, use your wit

Keep it at bay and away, to enjoy a long life long heavenly stay

Nine years ago, I developed a theory, the fruition of which has been the 100% absence of any form of mental illness. Yes, all symptoms gone: zero burnouts, zero euphoria, delusions, paranoia and hallucinations. I am void of any long-term psychotropic medications or long-term psychotherapy. The return of creativity, abstract and logical reasoning, vivid memories and motivation define my mental status. Unbridled energy, enthusiasm and health define my physical state: the two are inseparable.

The theory embodies the need to challenge the brain and body, a return to community and enjoyment and the nourishment of the brain and body with correct nutrition. I wish to restore, then optimize, the biochemistry and neurochemistry of us all. The goal, optimal health, happiness, increased productivity and major reductions in the healthcare monetary drain.

Fortunately, part of *InfinitE/IQ* is humor, a component of both community and stimulation. With this noted, again, a quote my father often used to quip: "Son, I never make the same mistake twice. Three or four times, but never twice."

I mention it because of a phone call I made this morning. And while I stress the need to reduce stress, prevent cortisol production and save neurons, I have the perfect prescription to destroy brain cells. Pick up your mobile phone, call your local big box home improvement store and request to be routed to a particular store category—in search of a particular item. Post phone call, take your pulse, blood pressure and search your pixelated screen for the movie, *Bullet to the Head*.

With my point made, and the vent opened, it is time to pen the value of another component of *InfinitE/IQ*. That component is stimulation, and involves both mental and physical challenges. Physical challenge in the form of exercise and physical education in the home, workplace and educational system. I am prompted to do this because exercise was a key component for my recovery, and health maximization for me and all people. I am further prompted because my youngest child has entered kindergarten, and my eldest the first grade. I find the reduction of physical education to three days per week, in an attempt to facilitate advanced learning, a huge mistake. Certainly, the nutritional aspects of a better student, which I will discuss soon, need also to be considered.

I have titled Chapter 28: *Stop and Think: the Tortoise and the Hare*

Revisited, because I believe, in our haste to expand time for learning and working, we our missing the point of building a sound, healthy foundation for both children and adults. Feed and challenge the body correctly, and we will build a smarter, happier and more energetic student and employee—in and for the long run.

I would like to discuss just a few of the benefits of exercise, briefly describe my own views on forms of exercise and offer suggestions per educational institutions and the workplace.

Let me begin by describing how exercise contributed to my cure of OCD and maximization of health. The extraordinary health benefits of exercise on the human body have been well-documented. Systems improved and effected include cardiovascular, pulmonary, endocrine, neural and more. We have a milieu of less stress and better function. This, of course, is a very high-level summary, but let's speak about the brain and the magnificent effects of exercise on it.

Exercise increases the production of BDNF, a factor required for new neural growth. In taking DHA with the fish oil, combined with BDNF, you now have the components for new neural growth. BDNF's specific function is to sprout new dendrites between nerves or neurons: these dendrites the essence of learning. During a lifetime, one neuron can make 20,000 such connections with other neurons. The brain, like the body, adapts to good stress: for the body exercise, for the brain reading, studying, thinking and riddles.

With BDNF release and a bit of mental exercise and DHA from fish oil long-chain fatty acid cocktails, feel free to build a lightning fast, efficient, creative, analytical and problem-solving brain.

Exercise also releases neuropeptides called endorphins, released after intense exercise. There are more readily released after an anaerobic workout, such as weight training or sprinting, but aerobic activity of longer duration can accomplish this as well. My half-hour intense weight training work-outs, or a half hour of intense sprinting or walking provide me with this release. This type of release leads to stress reduction, and—of course—less cortisol production in the long-term. Again, as discussed, excess cortisol production is extremely deleterious to brain neurons. It should be noted meditation can also release BDNF, so if my environment does not facilitate exercise, or one has a physical impairment, there is another option.

Exercise lowers excess blood glucose and lowers insulin, which helps provide a steady uniform flow of glucose. As long as the exercise is not excessive, the above two components ensure cortisol is not excessive. For completeness, remembering our AA from egg-yolk biochemistry, insulin activates delta-5 desaturase enzyme, which leads to AA production. Very soon, when I discuss nutrition, we will expand on insulin and other relevant hormones effected by incorrect or proper nutrition.

Please note: the steady, constant supply of glucose to the brain is paramount to brain health. Glucose maintains adequate ATP in brain-neuron mitochondria, which pumps out excitatory neurotransmitters into surrounding glia cells for storage. Not enough glucose = toxicity to neurons. In addition, too much glucose can also be toxic, as neuron glucose receptors are very sensitive.

And, of course, the brain needs oxygen. As the cardiopulmonary benefits of exercise increases, so does brain health in turn.

It should be noted, eating correctly before and after exercise can greatly magnify all of the effects as well, along with DHA and EPA supplementation.

Proper exercise will also prevent what I like to call humankind's evolutionary weak link. This weak link has created a great deal of pain and suffering for many of us, and when this baby hurts, your brain can not function optimally. Yes, the cerebral hemispheres do not like constant chronic pain.

And so, six million years ago when *Sahelanthropus* went bipedal, the spine's evolution began. Now, I have surely touted the magnificence of the brain, but many of us are familiar with the desire for a better back. So, when 2.5 million years ago, *Australopithecus africanus* enjoyed its curved lower back design to absorb shock, many wish to say, "Dude, it's not working!" To make it work requires work, so folks, the best thing all of us can do is to foster an exercise program to add stability, and keep the weight off this region.

The above description of exercise only touches the very expansive list of exercise benefits: both aerobic and anaerobic. From a personal perspective, when I do not work out the effects are immediate and profound, and an immediate impact on mental and physical acuity occurs.

Any workout routine recommended comes with the need for a physical. With that said, the patient should discuss their exercise types and goals. I would like to note that of the exhaustive studies I partook in during medical school to successfully complete the two core science years necessary to take USMLE Part I exam, the nutrition class and the benefits of exercise to the patient lacked in detail and did not stress their importance. It, of course, is amazing to me today that the human dietary program remains undefined and argumentative, although I believe the research I have come upon is the most accurate thus far. My daughter's guinea pig's diet plan is more refined than many lessons on human nutrition.

The shame of these dietary ambiguities is they exist for political and monetary reasons, and not from decrements in science. We know biochemistry, and we know the effects on biochemistry. Therefore, how is it possible we cannot name the type, ratios and quantities of foods to maximize biochemical reactions and peak human performance? Surely some who read my book might have possible objections, and I will simply say, "If what I tout is incorrect, how is it possible I have been symptom-free for nine years, the prior thirty-one years are descriptive of my opening riddle. Any guesses?"

Personally, and again with a doctor's approval, my favorite and most effective type of workout is a thirty-minute attack, which encompass anaerobic and aerobic systems at once. On the anaerobic side, I employ super-setting and multi-muscle fiber angles of attack to maximize dormant stem-cell release and to recruit multi-layer musculature, while drawing maximum endorphin release. The training is often sports-specific, and as often as possible avoids static lifting of weights, while remaining cognitive of injury safety. Core building is paramount to filling the void of man's weak link, discussed further below. This type of workout understands the need for forty-eight to seventy-two hours of muscle healing and replication, and of variation of body and muscles parts. Of course, I perform variations on the above theme, but the overriding theme is the body responds to stress by building.

A tad of self-induced anger helps to begin this type of workout: i.e., find something or create something to be pissed off at until the endorphins kick in. There is no need for this attack to happen on every workout. Be cognizant of inflammation (body literally feels hot inside), and the occasional need to skip a workout.

Leaving politics aside, my recommendations per education is to revisit a five-day-per-week physical education program. My other recommendation is to make this education full of good stress. There is no reason, three times per week, why a student cannot exercise to a therapeutic cardiovascular stress-building level. The heart rate should be elevated for aerobic building for a minimum of twenty-five minutes. A student does not have to be athletic to perform well in gym class. Teachers need to set anaerobic and aerobic goals, and students need to attain them. Yes, grade them as you would any other class.

With this noted, and understanding the thirst for knowledge children have, there is an absolute need to educate our children early on and build upon this foundation—an expansive education on nutrition and exercise. These teachings need to spill over to the science classes, and yes, I am advocating early on anatomy, physiology and biochemistry classes, including sexual education. My child's dentist has more pull on setting firm health foundations than the public-school system. How is this possible? Our kids are in school a third of the day, five days per week, while they visit the dentist every six months for fifteen minutes. If you desire higher test scores, build a better mind and body with food and exercise of the right type. Yes, we need to spend the extra money to get the proper foods into the cafeterias of America and the world.

In a previous chapter, I described an absence on the baseball diamond of twenty years. About thirteen years ago, a friend from the old neighborhood called me up and asked me to pick up the glove and bat again. Do you know I had forgotten how to throw a baseball over those two decades? After the first practice, I went home and analyzed all I had known about the sport, and applied science to my retooling the sport. I stopped and rethought the sport from the ground up, and applied all I had learned: biophysics, physics, anatomy, exercise physiology, kinematics, food science, sports training and physical therapy concepts. Today, I throw with greater velocity and react with greater bat speed (note: I hit ninety-five MPH at age sixteen). That phone call by a friend has led me to teach baseball and softball today, and for the last ten years. Do not underestimate the capabilities of a child and your students. The brain is a sponge: feed it and nourish it. I hope to write about my ideas on training and exercise in a future and dedicated writing.

It is never too late to learn, and there is much to learn. My point: stop and think, study and absorb. If you are good, you can be better. None of us have all the answers. Yes, to all of us, keep asking questions—but also develop solutions. Think for yourselves as well.

The tortoise, despite the time involved, took the time to make nutritious meals and spent extra money on healthy food. No matter how busy the schedule, he took the time for daily exercise. The tortoise enjoyed his community and found time to relax. The tortoise understood more would be accomplished and enjoyed in his life, because he would have more energy, sustained health and longevity with this formula. So today, the tortoise strives to teach the hare this life lesson. The tortoise does this because he understands the whole of nature. Some form of this lesson was first described back in 600 BC., and I revisit it today for you, and as a reminder for me.

Open your heart, and let your emotions paint the pages with words of passion, inspiration and knowledge!

CHAPTER 29

THE ABYSS, BEDRIDDEN AND THE DOPAMINE WINDOW

Hello all. Yes Mr. Hornsby and Skaggs did it again this morning, on Track Three, 5:33, *Mandolin Rain*, "You don't know what you got, 'til you lose it all again." Actually, for me, on that drive back from Chicago, viewing the flat, endless Indiana farmland, I did know what I had, as I had it taken away so many times before. What I needed was a solution, not a reminder.

As you recall, I opened this book with this Letter to The Reader: the reason to remind all to live life to the fullest. Again I will repeat it.

Dear Reader,

When was the last time you took notice of young toddlers at play and witnessed the joy, love, innocence, fire for learning, void of inhibition and infinite energy they exude: a sight that just left you chuckling with a friend?

Or when was the last time you laid down on a forest floor on a cool summer's eve and listened to the canopy's opera of chattering birds, just prior to the silence that ensues when the sun finally sets, and nature grants permission to rest?

And so, I awoke this morning, then pounded the body a half hour hard, kicked in the endorphins and let the BDNF fly wild. The DHA converted to more neuronal dendritic connections, enabling me the courage to pen the difficult chapter that follows.

I had watched the tricyclic antidepressant/MAO inhibitor combination run me into burnouts, and now my mind was propelled into a hallucinatory-psychotic break medical-school-term-ending event. My life environment would now take over. The inability to extinguish the timeline from age fifteen to this point was hard to delete from my cerebral hemispheres. I came back only to have it taken away, time and time and time and time again. For thirty-one years, I would fight. Then one day, I followed a notion, and found a magic potion. I would call the potion *InfinitE/IQ*; the notion, *The Lindemann Theory*.

When I completed the last years at my New Jersey university academic institution, burnout free, I thought these events were a thing of the past. When I developed *The Lindemann Theory* and took a retrospective analysis of those last collegiate years and my studies, I realized I did not bartend on weekend nights. The significance became relevant.

During those days and the bartending job I had, the work was a nonstop seven-hour shift, making and serving customers drinks, six people deep all night. While I loved the physical workout of those nights, those shifts were pretty exhausting. And so, with this rigorous load eliminated, cortisol stress levels and the will (and medicated overdrive) to override them were absent—thus the void in burnouts. Had I not been on medications and instead had *InfinitE/IQ* in action, a simple Sunday afternoon on the couch would have sufficed in recovery. Evidence for this: I have nine years of it right now!

At the time, there was no way to comprehend this, as it was not examined correctly. Let me make this point again. Today, while medication and symptom-free, if I perform exhausting work I may suffer like everyone else, but I will only need one-half to one day to simply lie in bed to recover. The burnouts I had during these events were four to six weeks long, and left no chance to recover at school and work.

And so, the thoughts of lost time, money, a delayed career and disrupted life pervaded my mind in '90 and '91. They took their toll. The result was a gradual, then rapid descent to an abyss. I would experience my first major and long clinical depression. Understand, when I overdosed on the experimental drug, as previously mentioned, there were depressive qualities at play. But the majority of the need to escape was because of the sheer, agonizing, nonstop pain from the obsessions. In terms of raw pain, there was nothing worse than the state of nonstop obsessions.

You label pain on a scale of one to ten, and with vivid, horrid honesty the state of OCD for me sent that scale to fifteen—stress, anxiety and exhaustion off the charts. Clinicians, please understand this! Certainly, there was one exception and that was the demonizing walk in the winter storm, when I escaped the mental health facility. That one night eclipsed all on the mental pain scale. The pain was not just excruciating, it was so very, very, deep—the word deep brings tears to my eyes. I won't let anyone get there—I'll do my best.

With that noted, the state of clinical depression is extremely painful, both mentally and physically. Yes, physically. Odd, right? Let me be frank, at the worst of this depression, I was bed ridden for six months. Yes, I only got out of bed for meals, and I simply could not move. My parents were beside themselves, as I had to move back home, and they had to watch their son be bedridden. There was a void of energy unlike anything I had experienced before. My body ached with unexplained pains. My mind was dull and achy—void of obsessions—just in an achy, torpid, useless state.

For completeness, the burnouts had no physical or mental pain component, but rather a frustrating, confusing and exasperating void of energy. Yet, I remained cognizant that pushing through did and would delay the recovery process. In burnout mode, when I approached the tasks that sent me to this state—such as going to sit at my desk to study—I actually felt repulsion to the activity. It was almost like two magnets of similar polarity being propelled away from each other.

In a previous chapter, I redefined the standard definition of OCD. While I am tempted to do so for the word depression I will not, and for this reason. Depression can be a slow creeper. It can start with ruminating negative thoughts and slowly advance to the state I just described: flat-out, full-blown, bed-ridden clinical depression. The goal, obviously, is to prevent the advancement to this state: so people, parents and clinicians beware. Act early, rather than later. The means of clean fuel, community and stimulation I utilize today maintain health; they should be your weapon of prevention.

The depression was taken to another level of devastation, when it became evident, time-wise, I would not be able to return to medical school in the fall of 1991. Now I would be two years behind. Add on all the university delays and time was simply slipping into a futuristic abyss. I kept thinking about it: *Time is slippin', time is slippin'*, and the deeper I went. As I sunk deeper, there was the omniscient shadow of, "How do I prevent the events of burns and highs from coming back?"

Despite being bedridden with a severe clinical depression, my parents managed to get me into the car, and I was introduced to a Dr. Gorall at the Belle Mead, New Jersey Mental Health Facility. Dr. Gorall, a fine, pleasant physician, reviewed my history and prescribed a new medication. This pharmaceutical was void of SSRI, but rather possessed a mechanism of action on the neurotransmitter dopamine.

It is a strong inhibitor of the dopamine-reuptake system, and it also downregulates beta-adrenergic function. It does stimulate the central nervous system, with possible nervousness and insomnia. Mania is described as a possibility, but no mention of burnouts. Again, before this writing I was unaware of the mania possibility.

And so, I slept in bed, in the riddled hell described in Chapter 28 and waited for dopamine receptors to change—and I hoped. Weeks later it would happen, a dawn in me. The absolute removal of all symptoms took place. Just as the OCD-effective drugs removed all obsessions, the medication removed all symptoms, physical and mental, of this bout of clinical depression. The obsessions were also gone. To reiterate, when any medications worked on either obsessions or this case of depression, it was an all-or-none recovery for me. The absence of symptoms were by no means gradually reduced; they were there one day, and when the long-term receptor changes were invoked—I presume—the symptoms were gone.

In addition, there was a very nice benefit of the medication. It allowed for an orgasm and ejaculation. This is significant because the human orgasm can be very health-beneficial as a stress and anxiety reducer, as well as a mood elevator. Known increases in dopamine, oxytocin, prolactin and androgen receptors can occur. Stress reduction is always a part of any wellness program, so the elimination of the inability to orgasm was significant, and allowance of the neurochemistry of sex as an adjunct was much welcomed. By no means, though, did it ever occur to me to secede from a medication because of this side effect: the benefits far outweighed this concern.

So, an abyss and hell were entered, I found a window again, and I explored a new set of neurochemical alterations. Were we done with burnouts and hallucinations? What about depression? Well, let me avoid delay and ruin the suspense, stating unequivocally, "No, we were not done." It tears me and tears me to tell you, I still had another eighteen years of chaos before the rainbow and *The Lindemann Theory* reached fruition. But the rainbow would come for me, and this book will be complete for others.

With employment at the family business for income, plans began for re-admittance to medical school. The summer of 1992, on July 27th, marked a new semester, and another drive out west to begin a new chapter. Let the summer of 2017 set me free! Let me finish this book, in hopes of setting others upon a rainbow.

There is nothing wrong, but everything right with hope!

CHAPTER 30

COMPLETION, AND TIME KEEPS ON SLIPPIN'

Good morning, all. Today is going to be my best day ever!

It was just a slow, relaxing jog and mellow swim this morning. The latter had me netting soaking acorns, already in the process of leaching tannins into the pool's concrete bottom. While my advice on the avoidance of "ghost whisperers" in dating was limited, so too is my advice in pool design. Of course, I would not suggest owning a pool with a 100-foot eastern black oak right above it, as do we. Cut it down? Never! This *Quercus velutina* is a thing of beauty, and when that red hawk sits at the apex of the tree's crown, it's purely majestic. Two weeks ago, a woodchuck managed a huge bite out of the trunk's base. The tree bled sap for three days straight: the early release of tiny acorns—a sign of illness: followed by repair and then healing.

This morning's workout was by no means the normal heavy intensity that warrants my body to come alive and release growth hormone (GH), thyrotropin (TSH), prolactin (PRL) and endorphins from the brain's anterior pituitary gland, and vasopressin (ADH) from the posterior pituitary—all from the master gland beneath the base of the brain.

Meanwhile, while the brain spills, the adrenal cortex pumps out cortisol and cortisone with epinephrine anti-inflammatory effects and aldosterone: the adrenal medulla epinephrine and NE is driven by hypothalamic nerves. Remember, NE was being acted upon by my medications. Perhaps exercise can help replace this action? *The Lindemann Theory, the powerful triad of InfinitE/IQ,* twenty-nine years of schooling and thirty-one years of clinical history, experience and research thinks perhaps so.

Elsewhere in the body, with stressful or prolonged exercise we see thyroxine (T4) and triiodothyronine (T3) released, as well as insulin, glucagon, testosterone, estrogen, progesterone and Renin.

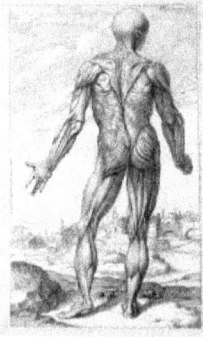

Above is a pretty interesting list of increased exercise-induced secretions. The answer to the question, "Can exercise have an effect on the body?" becomes a resounding, "Yes." Remember folks, all of these are hormones, and hormones act to alter rates of cellular reactions. How many cells are in the human body? Trillions is the answer. The word stress is a dichotomy only to the uninformed. The right stress upon the human body sets it free and makes it alive, the wrong stress drains and strains the life force. Let's become informed!

Add the effect of fueling these trillions of cells properly with clean fuel, and we have a powerful means to regulate human biochemistry and neurochemistry. While this morning's run was less intense, it provided me an opportunity for expansive thought. It allowed me to draw a simple analogy to ease understanding of *The Lindemann Theory* for my reader.

To serve as a guideline for the remainder of this book and for life, please picture a pot of barely simmering hot water: the recipe a simple hard-boiled egg. Let the simmering water represent the normal baseline (balance) of the human brain's neurochemistry, the neurons firing away and dendrites exploding in communication. At a slow, hot simmer, the brain is an efficient machine: creative, logical and full of massive reasoning power. Picture the simmering water as a neurotransmitter bath, in perfect balance for the brain it nourishes. The bath is a balance created and evolved over 500 million years of hormonal evolutionary history and five million years of modern human evolution history. A complex, intricate bath, that explodes at adolescence—in complexity—before it settles.

Adding a substance to a fine, effective balance such as this one can generally affect the balance in one of two ways: bring the baseline up or bring it down. For purposes of illustration, it is known alcohol (ROH) will decrease the boiling point of water, thus making the water easier to boil: it elevates above baseline. If you add too much ROH, the water could boil over the pot. We will equate this overboil to the psychological phenomenon of paranoia, delusions, hallucination, mania and psychosis. Too many mood elevators, natural highs of life paired with mood-elevating drugs or a change in lifestyle, might boil over or end in mania. For me, personally, the overboil equated on two occasions to an escalating off-euphoric feeling, ending in an event of approximately one hour where "euphoria shifted to delusions and hallucination, followed by an off-the-shelf, full-blown psychosis, an emergency room visit and subsequent career and life-altering event.

On the other hand, salt is known to increase the boiling point of water, making the water harder to boil. If one adds salt to a nice simmer, you will get a flat line and drop below baseline. And so, we can equate salt to cortisol burn out: reduced neurotransmitter balance and depression.

Changes, including diet and long-chain fatty acids (from a bad diet to a good diet) and exercise, coupled with mood elevators, will equalize the boil.

So, nine years ago, I looked at my thirty-one-year history, and analyzed deviations to the baseline. Please keep the above simmering pot of water analogy in mind as I finish my story, and then reach and present my final—but no means complete—conclusions and recommendations. I so thank you thus far for hanging in there with me, but—as the black oak bled—we have a bit more bleeding in this chapter, before we heal.

Make no mistake about it. I did go on to complete the first two years of medical school: the core science years all physicians complete, which are the two most difficult years folks speak of when they hear about medical school. The material was fascinating. The courses studied and completed included these: pathology, clinical neuroscience, pharmacology, microbiology and immunology, physiology, biochemistry, clinical anatomy, molecular cell biology, human genetics, embryology, medical ethics, biostatistics, microscopic organology, psychosocial factors in medicine, preventive medicine, nutrition, cardiopulmonary resuscitation, introduction to clinical medicine and a fellowship project in cardiac resuscitation.

The path was arduous, as the problem was never resolved. Yes, the burnouts would create interruptions again. These interruptions coupled with normal medical school life events: my first-ever failed class: pathology. (I later retook the course in Kansas City with success.) Then, a first failed attempted passage of USMLE Part I, the test required to move on to years three and four, led me into the winter of 1997. Let's start with my arrival back to medical school, after a devastating depression.

I arrived back to medical school and began again in July of 1992, and suddenly it was February of 1997, and I was retaking USMLE Part I. Remember, this all started back in September of 1981 in North Carolina. Suddenly, almost sixteen years after the start of my graduate work, I found myself about to take USMLE Part I for the second time. I had been through the return of obsessions, the failure of an experimental drug, burnouts, a psychotic break, a suicide attempt and a major depression. In 1997, I would find myself a decade and one half down the road—a road unlike the yellow brick road.

The worst part of this marathon was the nagging thoughts of an unsolved equation. When or how would it hit next, would the simmer spill over—or would it flat line? It was 1976, America's fabulous bicentennial year, when the Steve Miller Band penned and sung "Fly Like an Eagle". The lyrics started to ring in my ears in 1997, *Time keeps on slippin', slippin', slippin' into the future, time keeps on slippin', slippin', slippin' into the future …*

When would I be free?

Unquestionably, I had let my spirit carry me, and I persevered under extraordinary circumstances. I met fantastic folks including students, professors, administrators at this Illinois medical school. I was even taken in by a wonderful family out of Libertyville, Illinois, the mother of which just passed away a month ago—cancer again. They are wonderful people whom I stay in contact with today; they continue to motivate me to write, conclude and fight.

I had just finished a board's review class and was set to take the test. From university and medical school, I had grown accustomed to test groups of 100 to 200 people. By 1997, my medication list had grown exponentially, one bad patch upon another: uppers, downers and all-arounders. I even had a major tranquilizer in my bloodstream in 1997. I was seeing not only a psychiatrist for a medication review, but attending weekly psychotherapy meetings with another gentleman—the cost and time was yes, *crazy*. Actually, the peak of the abyss, if an abyss can have a peak, was the day my psychiatrist asked if maybe I should seek handicap status. Yep, how's that for a solution. It left me numb.

And again, I reiterate, there was no discussion of the core medicine causing oscillating effects, or of augmenting dosages down: a non-discussion for thirty-one years. And, of course, there was the continuation of a medication that would cause permanent—yet thankfully non-progressive—damage to my kidneys.

I woke up, and walked over to the campus of the medical school in February of 1997. I was prepared for the exam, with no thoughts of what was to happen next—absolutely and honestly none. While the preceding paragraphs explain the event causation, I had no cognitive awareness it was in the future for me. The administrator of the exam was actually the gentleman who ran the prep course for USMLE Part I. He was a great guy, and it was nice to see him. I was then led to this very tiny room. I was the only one there, which caught me off guard. I was handed a number two pencil, and awaited the start of the exam—bold circles to be made on questions covering some incredible material.

I was given the go ahead. It was baffling, but I felt the most incredible void—a lonely feeling—and then the words slippin, slippin, and lost, lost time started to resonate. I looked at the first question and simply stared. I put the pencil down and stared some more and some more, and then I simply stood up and looked at my proctor for the exam and said, "That's it."

He said, "Rob, are you sure? Rob?" in desperation. I could see the pain in his face.

Almost sixteen years, to leave with nothing, and I said, "That's it.". There was a micro second of joy.

And so, in February of 1997, I walked away. It was a voluntary withdrawal. The medical reasons were laid out pretty vividly.

In 2009, some twelve years later, I solved the equation by myself. *The Lindemann Theory* was born. I want to walk back in.

For anyone who has ever asked me why I left medical school and I rambled on, please read my book. As you can see, it is not a simple answer. It is a painful question that brings all to the fore every time it is asked. As the black oak bled, I depart this chapters with not just tears, but a very hard cry—a real hard cry. The rainbow has come already in the form of health, family, community and help for all, if they consider *The Lindemann Theory* and consider *InfinitE/IQ*, a formula for near boundless energy and cognition.

Let me stop the bleeding, once and for all. Let me back into medical school: if not for me, for others. Let me fly like an eagle. Realize, everyone—please, there is nothing wrong, but everything right with hope. Realize it and embrace it!

Open your heart, and let your emotions paint the pages with words
of passion, inspiration and knowledge!

CHAPTER 31

ESCALATING EVIDENCE FOR THE LINDEMANN THEORY

Good morning, all. Today is going to be my best day ever!

The slow simmer of yesterday of hard-boiled eggs left an easy peel and cold-water wash in the "prep" of my morning breakfast. The arachidonic-acid-laden yolk was tossed, and the filling was designed for eight halves of hard-boiled eggs. I cut, crushed and rolled romaine, scallions, green peppers, grape tomatoes, and cilantro into an already-prepared guacamole blend, and spooned prodigious dollops into the protein receptacles.

A quick peel of some young healthy clementines left my breakfast complete, the contents by design to target a ratio of protein to carbohydrate to fat I find optimal on intake. The quantities and types of those macronutrients, and the significance of this ratio, can leave me at dawn feeling like a nine versus a groggy six.

Kick in some intense exercise, some long-chain fatty acids, some community and love and challenges in mind and career, and kick it up to a ten-plus. *The Lindemann Theory* leads to a way of life, which I'll denote as *InfinitE/IQ*. Soon to complete the evidence supporting *The Lindemann Theory* and soon to elaborate on *InfinitE/IQ* stimulation, clean fuel and community, let us first take a ride with my children to the Jersey Shore, and a stroll down memory lane.

With the Lindemann girls ready to roll, we packed the hybrid and headed to Belmar, New Jersey for a dip into the Atlantic: the building of castles adorned with shells and polished surf stones, and strolls along the new, post-Hurricane Sandy boardwalk.

I reflect back to my glory days, the year 1970, the vehicle—the family station wagon with Mom at the helm. It was called suntan lotion, not sun block, and the radio was ablaze with hot tunes. I was young, but I have to admit the funk of "Spill the Wine" performed by Eric Burdon and War, combined with the flavor of coconut tanning lotion, would have had any prepubescent testosterone flowing.

And so, the hot sexy lyrics went, and the groove was set ...

There were long ones, tall ones, short ones, brown ones, black ones, round ones, big ones, crazy ones, out of the middle came a lady, she whispered in my ear, something crazy, she said, spill the wine, take that pearl, spill the wine, take that pearl...

Only to be followed by "Ride, Captain, Ride" recorded by Blues Image.

Ride, captain, ride upon your mystery ship, Be amazed at the friends you have here on your trip, Ride, captain, ride upon your mystery ship, On your way to a world that others might have missed ...

Once sand bound, the rocky jetty was the target, where starfish, crabs and crustaceans of all kinds intrigued me. The building of those jetties, post-World War II, reminds me of my father and his brothers—my uncles. Raised in Jersey City, New Jersey, all four brothers, Charlie, Richie, Willie and Robert would enter that war. My father, Robert, the youngest, would enter at age eighteen. The other three brothers would see horrific action, all four would return alive. It was the post WW II plan that allowed my father to enroll at the Newark College of Engineering, and to purchase a home and start a family in Central, New Jersey.

Certainly, it was the mystique and allure of cigarettes taken up during those years, which may have led all to pass away from cancers of different types. You have to ask though, how cool is a substance containing over 5,000 chemicals? Yes, ten million smokers are expected to die per year by 2025. Yes: ten million *human beings* per year. Pardon the pontificating side note, but I could not help myself: the book's purpose is you.

Rhaena and Rochelle were grooving and rocking to different tunes as we traversed the Garden State Parkway. For them, the hybrid was ablaze with Alecia Keys "Girl on Fire", and I played DJ on Enrique Iglesias tracks.

The girls would scream, "Daddy, number one, number four, number five!"

We arrived at a beautiful, newly constructed boardwalk; Hurricane Sandy destroyed the wooden splinters I had grown up with as a kid. The girls walked the composite decking and barefooted onto massive white sandy beaches, dotted with wonderful new playgrounds for the children. Rochelle, the five-year old, would take the first wave to a tumble, and we all held hands and welcomed the salty Atlantic.

I reflected back to that night of 2012 when Superstorm Sandy hit: a storm taking over 200 lives and creating a seventy-five-billion-dollar loss in havoc. I sent my girls to North Jersey to stay with Rosanne's parents: my concern, the massive trees overlooking our home. With the electricity out, I proceeded with a flashlight in hand, to put in a wood floor on our house's top floor. An intelligent choice? By no means, no. But I did calculate if the ninety-foot oak did drop, if would fall five feet short of my body. Truth is, I was simply trying to dismiss anxiety during this very, very strange storm. All was aligned that night: the stars, tides, winds and chaos in the skies. I sat through a hurricane in Florida, but this was no ordinary storm: let me describe it.

It was about ten p.m. Curiosity and adventure driven, I ventured outside with my hammer in one hand, flashlight in the other. All electric was out, and would remain so for the next two weeks. I walked to the middle of the yard and stood in a hurricane with minimal rain, at least for my location. And then I looked up at the trees and watched them bending in half: all except the mighty black oak. There in the night, I witnessed the most eerie, powerful surges of wind I had ever seen. By all means, it was not a steady wind, but rather massive, potent surges—one surge followed by another, and broken by calms of ease and unease, as I awaited the next rush. A neighbor joined me; we were mesmerized by the invisible power in the air, the cloak broken as we listened to snapping trees all around us. I watched as a massive limb entered my next-door neighbor's roof, a small hole for him, but for others not so.

With no intent on creating a biblical metaphor, it was as if a massive hand was sweeping back and forth. I imagine the power stroke creating the massive whoosh, the reset stroke leaving a bewildering calm. And while I listened, my brother-in-law, just fifty miles north, watched water rise and bury his home in a matter of minutes—a collapsing dyke the source of hysteria, the town of Moonachie buried.

And with Sandy pondered, it is time to visit another storm and complete my story. I proceed with excitement. When I walked outside that hurricane night, my anxiety lifted, as I entered the known—leaving the unknown of a dark, enclosed house. And so, as I bear all my knowns and my soul to you, the relief and joy to help others will set me free. The misconceptions, the misinterpretations—not just buried to a chasm—but cleansed by reality and education. Sixteen years to complete some six-plus years of school, I have to listen to people call me a drop-out. Do it to my face, and I'll drop you in a second!

"Losing" close to sixteen years was extraordinary to grasp. The toll of departing medical school, aside from absolute dismay included a body that was sixty-five pounds overweight. My blood chemistry panel had gone awry, two kidneys had been unknowingly damaged, and my medication list had grown inexplicably out of control. It was then noticed I had developed sleep apnea, and I sought a specialist to solve it. Not knowing then what I know now about obesity, the effects of inflammation and a biochemical storm, certainly a loss of weight may have been a likely alternative to the prescribed tonsillectomy. That option was neither offered nor discussed. I am left to leave it at that, I suppose, or certainly feel free to expand in thought after reading the concluding chapters on my historical overview, *The Lindemann Theory* and a final summation of *InfinitE/IQ*.

A colleague of mine just noted to me, sadly, that the summer of 2017 is almost over, yet I smiled and jested back we have a quarter of summer left. And so, I am only left to put a positive spin on a tonsillectomy gone wrong, and leave the reader with one more bit of evidence to reflect on.

It was to be a quick procedure, a recovery with a tad of ice cream as therapy. My goal was to reach optimum performance for the job I had taken out in Chicago right after medical school. Well aware of the significance of sleep in restoring the nervous system's insulation, broken down during the day, the decision to correct the apnea was an easy one. The result bordered on the bizarre. Writing today, I am still at a loss of what finally occurred, so perhaps you the reader might help me?

And so, with anesthesia given, I was to have my first operation. I looked forward to having my apnea corrected. My new, sleeping brain would produce cells which would repair and grow myelin around nerve cells. I was already doing extremely well at my new job, a few days off, was well worth becoming number one, not just number two in the company at an important task.

I awoke from the operation and anesthesia and was seated in a hall. I nurse came over to me, and asked me to lift my head up. I had a towel over my head, grasping it with two hands, my throat and head absolutely screaming in pain. As the nurse showed me a series of photos to describe my pain, I picked the one showing the absolute highest level of pain. The nurse knew immediately I had awoken from an operation void of pain medication, a major anesthesia mistake the most likely cause. She was furious. I was immediately admitted back into the hospital, and administered intravenous pain medication. As a side note of coincidence, when I did follow up after returning home for causation of error, I was told the anesthesiologist retired.

Once medicated, I explained to hospital staff the need to arrive at a scheduled work seminar, and I was accommodated with the discharge. The timing was such that I would just make the event, with no time to pick up my prescription. Unaware at how fast the pain medication would leave my system, forty-five minutes into the event, my head was again on fire.

The next day I awoke expecting to be fine, and instead I was plunged into one of the burnouts I had experienced before. As I theorized in 2009, I believe these fatigue episodes to be explained as follows. An already overtaxed adrenal cortisol system by the existing medication cocktail was pushed to the limit via an abnormal pain event. My normal recovery mechanism to stress was disabled or overridden. A four-week burnout followed.

I met with my employer and explained the operation mishap.

They understood, and it was explained to me I would still receive a very important list despite the interruption. In the line of work I was doing, this list represented my ability to succeed for an entire year, both performance and commission-wise, so it was tremendously important.

It was unexpected for me and the employer that the days missed would extend four weeks. I returned to work with an apology, and offered to return four weeks in salary and to resume my work load. The manager of the office remarked with attitude he could care less, he was not paying the bill. Contrary to his word, he removed my list so vital to me succeeding for a full year.

It was a Friday. An employee in my group, upon leaving for the weekend, told me one of the people I had been working with was placed: the result was a commission. I simply responded, "Yes."

The following Monday I arrived at work, and members of the office started to file into a side meeting room. I was unaware of what was occurring. You're going to love this one, folks. And so, as I started my work schedule, I watched two police officers come into the main office. They asked me to pack my things and leave the office. Honestly, the event was so bizarre, I was left to chuckle. Absolutely at a loss, it was the final event leading me back to New Jersey. Still, I am at a loss to explain it fully to this day; yes, I feel it necessary to clear the air. The police officer actually revealed the absurdity of the event in his facial expression. It is said there are two sides to every story, please let me know the other; there was none. Generalities can be useful and dangerous at the same time. Again, there was only one side to this story.

And so, being second in the company in a task, a desire for better performance with a simple operation, botched anesthesia, a retired anesthesiologist, an early discharge to return to a work event, an illness of four weeks, an offering of returned salary and a major broken promise to majorly effect one year of performance somehow equaled two police officers and a loss of income.

I held my head high, shook the police officers' hands with warmth and mutual understanding, and returned to the family business in New Jersey. I left Illinois with another piece of final evidence to support my theory surrounding a vulnerable cortisol-adrenal-brain axis while under the influence of mood boosters. Certainly, the story provides valuable data to provide statistical reasoning for the proposed JAFA mental health unit described earlier. And reason to speculate this company had become privy to my medical history—and misinterpreted it?

All is good though. The journey to health is upon us. In the next chapter, I will utilize my education to research a means to lose sixty-five pounds and restore my biochemistry; the books will open again. The final pieces of the puzzle are to follow. Health will be achieved. A theory fulfilled. Love and family will develop, nurture and be cared for. An internal flame will not be extinguished and I will fight—and fight hard—for what is just and right. I will fight to be your physician because the essence of man and woman is not just "me". The essence of man is more importantly "YOU".

I will seek out reentrance to medical school, to complete a test validating my two successful, completed years, and resume my clinical training. It is what is just for me. It was what is just for you. My experiences in life are dramatic, scientifically important and clinically important. I desperately want to share my understanding of humility, empathy and the value of health and life.

I hope you will fight with me, so I can further fight for you. Remember all, please, there is nothing wrong, but ...!

There is nothing wrong, but everything right with hope!

CHAPTER 32

FUEL AND CHEMISTRY: THE FINAL PIECES

Good morning, all. Today is going to be my best day ever!
InfinitE/IQ's stimulation necessitates a good riddle:

Part of the Ancient Mariner Rime it is Not
Ghandi Nixed it for Twenty-one Days
I Choose Not
Do it Right, Live Real Ripe
Do it Wrong, Pay the Price
What Goes in, Must Come out
If Abuse, May Bind a Knot
Enjoy it, Though, it Satisfies
Understand it, and Multiple
Disrespect, your Genes May Fly
What am I, the Riddle Asks?
Open wide, and Name the Task

It would take a full four years before those thoughts of sixteen
lost years would finally catch up with me. In 2001, I was unable to
shake them, and the depression hit hard. It hit so very hard. I was
well aware there was little time to find a new medication to work.

Admitted to the Belle Meade, New Jersey Mental Health Facility, it was here you have already read about my escape, suicidal ideation and my only savior—a tree that had run out of limbs. The ECT unit would save my life, offering a total escape from depression. The fight was back on.

In February of 2002, I realized those sixty-five extra pounds were unwanted. I began to research the concept of dieting, and came upon some research with a sound scientific edge to it. Using my sixteen years of knowledge of the human body, I validated the biochemistry, neurochemistry and physiology, and pursued a food program whose reasoning I was able to confirm. Food and eating correctly satisfy the riddle; let us learn to do it right.

I will retain the total details of the food and body connection for a later writing. Here, we will explore a summary of food, now to be called fuel. It is part of *InfinitE/IQ's* clean fuel component. A beginning understanding rests in basic concepts of the mechanism of satiety, which exists in human beings today. Of course, it developed over five million years of modern human evolution. Food regulation or what makes "us full" to say, "No more food," has physiological checks, hormonal checks and timing checks. A quick lesson in physiology will begin the crash course. The hypothalamus, the amygdala and cortical areas of the limbic system all play a crucial role in the drive to eat, the hunger centers and satiation ("I'm full") — in a nutshell, control of human feeding.

An interesting side note, if one has a very unpleasant reaction to a food, an association is formed in the hypothalamus and amygdala can squash any further desire for that food. My own observation of my youngest daughter's stomach flu at age two, where vomiting by coincidence began right after the ingestion of a banana, left her to avoid the fruit for three full years. Only recently have we been able to have her eat a half a banana, where before this was her favorite staple. Let's expand on the brain connection.

With that phenomenon confirmed, I pray daily to my maker that I, too, would have a similar occurrence with cookies—any cookie. Speaking of cookies, let's talk about glucose a bit. Drops in blood glucose levels will stimulate the hunger center in the ventromedial nucleus. This is a big connection, as we will soon explore the need to eliminate fluctuations in blood glucose and how to do it. Increases in amino acids in the bloodstream, the breakdown products of protein, tell us we are full. Fat entering the duodenum causes the release of cholecystokinin, a hormone which tells us to stop eating.

When our gastrointestinal tract becomes distended, the stomach and duodenum send inhibitory signals through the vagi, and via somatic sensory signals, to tell us we are full. Thus, an understanding of food surface area and solid versus semi-solid versus liquid meals becomes important. And with this said, the bulk size of food plays an important role in the speed and timing of breakdown, and absorption to the bloodstream. With speed of absorption being important, rate of meal consumption becomes important. If the family meal involves a speedy gorge to get to the next appointment, it is better to simply carry your meal and slowly pick at it. The latter choice is better. It allows natural feedback mechanisms to satiety centers, distension receptors and hormonal communication, to naturally tell us we are full.

Previously we discussed how we can override the cortisol control mechanisms, exasperated via exogenous mood boosters. Certainly a strong analogy exists to overriding natural centers of food control. A rapid and massive gluttonous partaking leaves the human with little chance of feeling a productive feedback response: "Hey, you are full, put down the fork." Instead, the feedback response is a massive, fatiguing bloat, and leads to a brain fog. The caloric intake is so excessive, the body is left no choice but to convert the excess to fat. I will have to reserve the latter conversion, and reasons thereof, to a latter writing.

Without delving into further scientific proof to the above explanation on satiation, let us examine a common-sense perspective on the human being and food control: one which I hope you'll extrapolate in thought throughout this reading. Human beings have been evolving for five million years. Again, the base hormonal systems have evolved for 500 million years. For the majority of existence man hunted and gathered, eating along the way. Our physiological mechanisms adapted and evolved to that lifestyle. Certainly, if you disrespect this notion, perhaps you are an entirely new species—and that should be examined.

With fuel feedback mechanisms briefly covered, let us examine the nature of the fuel. Macronutrients include protein, carbohydrates and fat. When taken in the correct proportions, and the correct types, they can dictate a day of bliss and productivity, versus a day of sludge and no desire to budge.

And so, we are not just speaking about clean fuel components, we are talking about a clean combination of the three: protein, carbohydrates and fat. Rather than reserve the following statement for the end of this very brief macronutrient food control summary, I would simply like to state my belief there is one correct way to eat, with minor variations, concerning an observation of genetic variation and malfunction.

There's one correct way to eat to reach optimal performance, optimal health and optimal longevity. Weight loss and optimal weight is a given when one eats correctly. Can you lose weight in other ways, besides the below food recommendations? Yes, feel free to send your body into a ketonic storm, or perhaps halt the storm before it occurs by losing weight, while living with abnormal body chemistries and hormonal systems: this in reference to very high protein/low carbo-hydrate diets. From here the list goes on to pills and surgical interven-tion. Follow your doctor's orders, but be aware of long-term studies and effects of alternative means. The minor goal, if overweight, is to lose weight and maintain the weight; the major goal is to provide the cleanest fuel to offer your bodily systems maximum efficiency and minimal stress. When you minimize stress in the human body, you reduce the probability of chronic illness. A long-life void of chronic illness is very, very possible.

This brief fuel-control summary begins with the macronutrient carbohydrate. The goal is to eat nutrient-rich carbohydrates with the lowest glycemic indexes, and the proper proportion of protein and fat at each meal. The glycemic index has three components: chemi-cal composition of the sugars in the carbohydrate, the soluble fiber content and the fat content. The goal is to have the "final product" enter the bloodstream the slowest, to avoid having the pancreas re-lease too much insulin. When the body sends out too much insulin, the biochemical storm begins. In general, blood sugar levels drop and the body reacts and stores fat—and keeps it there. Here is what you need to remember!

We have three sugars that make up carbohydrates: glucose, fruc-tose and galactose. These three are all absorbed by the liver, but only glucose is released to the bloodstream to reach cells. Again, our goal is the sloth, not the rabbit, in terms of carbohydrates. Pasta, breads, cookies, cereals and ice cream are glucose-packed. The glucose hits the liver and is rapidly and immediately sent to the bloodstream. Fruits have fructose and galactose. They first have to be converted in the liver to glucose before being release into the bloodstream—a slothier, more desirous path.

Then we have fiber, another important component for sloth control. Fiber acts to slow the rate of entry of carbohydrates into the bloodstream. Yes, as soon as you smash, blend and liquefy and juice your carbohydrates, you override speed control.

To the point, what carbohydrates are best? Vegetables (except for carrots, corn and potatoes): cauliflower, broccoli, spinach, romaine lettuce, bok choy, eggplant, zucchini, arugula, tomatoes (actually a fruit), cucumbers, artichoke hearts and the list goes on ...

And fruits, berries (the darker the color, the better), peaches, apples, pears, grapes (resveratol in skin, as do berries-natural phenol), grapefruits, oranges, nectarines, tangerines, clementines and the list goes on ...

In regard to grains, breads and pasta, keep these at a minimum at your table. Barley, oatmeal (slow-cooked) and whole-grain rye breads are best. If you are trying to lose weight, and are prone to uncontrolled consumption, totally avoid them until your health is in control. Then re-introduce them slowly and monitor the effects. Do not take the word addicted lightly. When the body's insulin levels surge and spike, and you begin oscillating levels of this hormone, the thirst for carbs is real and rapid—make no mistake about it.

The carbohydrate summary is simple: eat the right ones, in the right quantity and don't squash them. Whole foods, low-glycemic indexes, fructose and galactose forms are better. Include lots of fiber. Now, here is the beautiful thing about low-glycemic, high-fiber vegetables and fruits. You can eat more of them at the meal, and allow those stomach and duodenum distension receptors to tell you enough.

You're going to love this, folks. How much more of the food? Well, if you are a gal, a typical recommended amount of carbohydrate at a main meal would equal ¾ of an English muffin. If you chose a low-glycemic option, such as chopped spinach, feel free to consume— guilt-free— eighteen cups of spinach in place of the ¾ muffin. As a guy, you can eat the whole muffin, and yep, twenty-four cups of chopped spinach. Now pay attention to this also. With chopped spinach, not only do you fill and distend the stomach and have its receptors say, "There is food in there, and there's enough." You consume the carbohydrate more slowly, through sheer quantity; and—of course—packed with more nutrients. The details of the science are fascinating, the rules are pretty simple. Do you have to follow the rules? No. But if you do, you live a better life and a longer life, and one with less chance of chronic disease. Maybe our healthcare system might work a little better.

I am going to take a shot at this last point a little later, and give a little support to a former NYC mayor and his idea. Remember, a healthier life means less stress on body systems, less cortisol production, more brain cells remain and more brain cell connections. The latter is a function of a desire to be more active mentally and physically, because of a healthier-created milieu for oneself. Eat right and think great.

While we are in brain-enhancing and building mode, and I sense the reader's need to breath, I was hoping to be so bold as to offer another one of my brain neuron crashers. Last night while watching an award show, a recipient gave an amazing acceptance speech. Like my big box phone call driving me to the movie, *Bullet to the Head*, I perceive at least 20,000 neurons died last night. The speech went like this …

What an amazing night, amazing people and an amazing era. I would just like to thank my amazing partner, whom was amazing last night as well in bed, my amazing parents, my amazing co-workers and my amazing fans. The adventure was amazing, the product simply amazing, everything all everything was amazing, my amazing maker, I find you amazing. The recipient was forced of stage, as they trickled in the song Amazing Grace.

And so I got out of bed, checked on my girls and sat at the kitchen table. I consumed three sleeves of cookies, unbridled and unchecked with the normal protein and fat of my milk. I wandered to the family room's big screen, searched for—and indeed—watched *Bullet to the Head.*

Okay, take a deep breath and head with me to the effects of those cookies, unaccompanied by the macronutrients protein and fat. Let's first discuss protein, and reclaim those twenty thousand neurons. Protein is composed of amino acids. Remember, these in the bloodstream help tell us we are full. Twenty amino acids in total, with nine of them not able to be produced by humans; therefore, we need to consume those nine in our diet. Aside from water, protein is more abundant in the body than any substance. It is in cells, enzymes, the immune system, muscles, skin, eyes, nails and more. If you eat too much protein at a meal, insulin levels rise to get rid of excess amino acids, and excess insulin takes the extra protein and converts it to fat.

Science has seen changes in fat cells, a result of this excess protein. Amazingly, that means these cells become much more active at keeping fat. So, we want the correct amount of protein at a meal. We have learned insulin acts on the liver, and muscle cells to grab glucose from the bloodstream and store it. It grabs amino acids as well, and—

like carbohydrates—stores glucose and amino acids as fat. Glucagon, which is stimulated by protein, releases stored carbohydrates in the form of glucose from the liver. So, when you eat sleeves of cookies without the protein in milk, you go to bed and expect your brain to be starved of glucose for a night's sleep. Remember, protein is needed to move glucose back into the bloodstream.

Not only is the need for both protein and carbohydrates at a meal important, but the amounts and ratio are as well. We are looking to optimize the "to and fro" mechanisms of insulin and glucagon. With this said, too many calories at a meal means excess stimulation of insulin, and the balance is lost again. Protein amounts depend on one's lean body mass, and their activity level as well. These details will be reserved for a later writing, but suffice it to say, total daily protein should be calculated with a carbohydrate-to-protein ratio set. It is but a matter of calculating quantities of carbohydrates.

Remember, we are going to seek lean meat protein sources as we seek to avoid the AA found in fatty cuts of meat. Arachidonic acid, as we have discussed, has deleterious effects in creating unbalance in a group of proto-hormones called eicosanoids. Direct ingestion of AA is an absolute no, as the human body needs clean fuel. Arachidonic acid leads to a stressed system, and the human body reacts to stress by producing cortisol. At certain levels and types of stress, cortisol kills brain cells in the hypothalamus.

To summarize, we are looking to balance the ratio of carbohydrates and protein at a meal. Here is a protein primer list for your convenience.

Protein List Choices-<u>Optimum</u>

- Fish—Scallops, shrimp, lobster (despite untrue reports of high cholesterol), salmon, mackerel, tuna, trout, grouper, crab or tilapia—the colder the water the fish lives in the better—they have more of the good fat, i.e., EPA

- Turkey—white meat is better than dark
- Chicken—white meat is better than dark
- Lean cuts of beef and pork—filet mignon (beef tenderloin), pork tenderloin and hamburger (8% fat or less-rarely find)
- Soy and Whey Protein
- Soy Meat substitutes—like soy breakfast sausages and soy crumbles
- Egg Whites

Fat is essential to the human body. As with carbohydrates and protein, the correct amount and the right amounts are crucial. It should be taken with both these macronutrients. Again, it is responsible for the release of the hormone cholecystokinin, an activator of satiation. A zero-fat diet leaves you walking around hungry all day. Also, fat in the meal slows the rate of entry of carbohydrates into the blood stream. While you seek to avoid AA, also keep saturated fat at a minimum, although some is needed. Saturated fat raises insulin levels and can lead to insulin resistance, and in turn Type II Diabetes. Some better fats are monounsaturated fats. This type of fat is said to be neutral on the set of chemical reactions AA was detrimental to. Some excellent sources of monounsaturated fats are cashews, macadamias, almonds, avocados, olive oil and canola oil.

The above is a primer on the clean fuel program I partook in. Again, I was sixty-five pounds overweight, suffered high blood pressure, and had an aberrant blood chemistry panel for starting points. I ended with a loss of sixty-five pounds and a complete reversal of my high blood pressure. I estimate optimization of bodily biochemistry and neurochemistry were in place, inflammation reduced, and energy was restored. I once again became enthusiastic about exercise, a component of life I'd missed for about twenty years. Part time I began to train athletes. I began to model in New York City and New Jersey. I dabbled in some acting and commercial work, and I found my mood to be elevated. I was still on the dopamine-enhancing medication.

All seemed in order, but I still was unaware at this time of my now-theorized cumulative effects of medication and life events. In this case, the life event or environmental change was entrance of clean fuel to my body, and a resultant biochemistry neuro-chemical change. A double whammy was in place. The final pieces of the puzzle were falling into place, including the evidence crucial in determining *The Lindemann Theory*.

The journey was long, painful and arduous, but the finish line is near and for you. The finish line is for my girls. The finish line is for me.

Open your heart, and let your emotions paint the pages with words of passion, inspiration and knowledge!

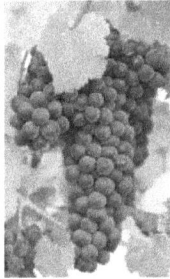

CHAPTER 33

THE SEA, FINISH LINES, REBIRTH AND THE RESCUE

G ood morning all. Today is going to be my best day ever! Let the summer of '17 set me free.

The year was 2002. The medication already described in my blood stream was already boosting mood via inhibition of norepinephrine and dopamine-reuptake mechanisms, and acting as a releasing agent of those two neurotransmitters. The clean fuel program was maximizing my hormonal and neurotransmitter biochemistry, and keeping insulin at minimum base levels. That minimum insulin level is fantastic, as insulin activates delta-5 desaturase, which leads to arachidonic acid formation, and in turn to undesirable proto-hormones. So, with insulin in check, my brain has that advantage; yours can also.

I also had plenty of glucagon circulating for the following reasons. It is known excess insulin can halt the production of glucagon, but with controlled insulin and a beautiful balance of carbohydrates, proteins and fats, glucagon is freely available. If there were not enough glucagon to release glucose for my brain, then cortisol is the body's back-up system to release stored glucose. But, at the same time, cortisol would destroy brain neurons if called upon too often. Aside from elucidating the body's back-up systems, we can now see in 2002 how beneficial a balanced insulin and glucagon network was for my brain, and can be for yours. With these hormonal connections made and treated with respect, we can very clearly see the formerly described double whammy effect from the prior chapter: mood booster (medication) + mood booster (clean fuel).

At the same time, the double whammy was in effect as my exercise routines continued, as described from a prior chapter. Let me remind you of the attributes of this *InfinitE/IQ* mechanism: exercise-induced physiological and neurological benefits. The type of exercise I was engaged in and continue to perform increases BDNF, which is needed for new neural growth, the sprouting of dendrites that enhance learning and creativity. Meanwhile, the exercise helped to lower excess blood glucose, and kept my insulin down. Remember, excess glucose can be toxic to neurons as well. Meanwhile, the brain loves oxygen; the cardiopulmonary effects of exercise ensure a wondrous O2 supply. When I complete my workout, I also personally experience a meditative effect (endorphin-induced, perhaps). It has been documented meditation can increase BDNF as well. What we have in effect is the ability to describe a new math equation:

Triple Whammy =
Mood Booster (Medications) + Mood Booster (Clean fuel) +
Mood Booster (Exercise)

And let us not forget, the prior described Type A personality, which perhaps might enhance the whammy to a four-fold whammy. With this stated and as a reminder, the Type A personality may also be more prone and likely to override body cortisol protection programs via drive and will.

During the same time, I introduced a fish oil concentrate containing high-dose EPA and DHA. DHA is a component for new neural growth, and BDNF is the factor which takes the DHA into new brain growth. I was already increasing BDNF with exercise, adding another ingredient for the recipe (BDNF + DHA) increased more of the final product: enhanced neuronal connections.

Meanwhile, the EPA I was consuming inhibited the delta-5 desaturase enzyme ("terrible zyme") that leads to undesirable hormones, and directed the path to better hormones. As a great side note, one of the better hormones we get is PGE1. It just so happens this baby (PGE1), while reducing insulin, leads to the synthesis of a large group of hormones known to decrease as we age. By doing so (increasing PGE1), we increase cAMP.

In effect, more PGE1 leads to more cAMP and the reversal of aging is in place. Okay, the last piece of good news is it is well-documented in laboratory animals that caloric restriction and clean fuel has major longevity attributes, so we can optimize the body. It allows DNA to be sustained longer: living longer with maximized health is the goal. Now, let me present the bad news (for me), but only for 2002. Well, actually for thirty-one years.

The equation just took on a factor of five. I had a quintuple whammy brewing in 2002.

Quintuple Whammy: Mood Boosters + Four=

Medication + Clean fuel + Exercise + Type A + Long-chain Fatty Acids (EPA AND DHA) =

"The Big Birds Nest: the Cuckoo's Nest Awaits" (to be the 2nd flight over)

I like good news though. The final Cuckoo's Nest would be the final piece of evidence to support *The Lindemann Theory*, and—of course— *InfinitE/IQ*, the powerful Triad of Stimulation, Community and Clean Fuel.

As with my entrance to medical school, I had that same off-euphoric feeling after the lifestyle changes of clean fuel, exercise and long-chain fatty acids took effect. There also existed some cognitive recognition of it; I was semi-aware things were off. It came to a head one night, when I went to a movie theater with a date. I was watching the feature, and I became entranced by the hum of the air conditioning unit above. As I felt sort of mesmerized by the hum, my brain went into a full-blown hallucination.

The thought process was as follows: the doctor in charge of my care was in trouble. I believed his home was on fire. I needed to save him. I needed to leave the movie and ask my date to find a ride home, and I needed to drive my car to the rescue. While en route to the rescue, I became aware I was in trouble, and drove to my parents' home. I asked my father to immediately drive me to the emergency room. I believe it was either when I was on the way, or while there at the E.R.—I went into full psychosis or unconsciousness; I do not remember.

I would like to note for the reader, the experience of delusion and hallucination for me had no level of mental pain to it (discomfort: the confusion and anxiety), but rather a small fight-or-flight reaction, as to a non-existent emergency. In the case of the medical school situation and the movie theater situation, it is interesting to note in both cases I felt someone else was in trouble. In medical school it was a kitten, and in the theater it was my doctor. A quick interpretation might be a displaced concern. Perhaps I knew someone was in trouble, that was—of course—me, and displaced it to another person.

In both cases, I would say the hallucination existed for about fifteen minutes before I recognized it to be such and sought help. There is very little doubt in my mind the episode was, in fact, attributable to my Five-Fold Quintuple Whammy Equation. This statement is borne out by nine years of symptom and medication-free living, the scientific explanations offered throughout this text, and the final summation and conclusions.

For completeness, I will note this hallucinatory event—and the lingering of thoughts concerning sixteen years of education and no MD degree—did require two more ECT treatment rounds in 2002 and 2005. I would come out healthy again. I did have one very scary reaction to one ECT treatment. I will not disclose the details of this, for several reasons. The causation was not explained, or not known, and I do not know how it was resolved. I believe it is safe to say a different brain center was unexpectedly activated. The good news is— despite it being an extremely scary situation for hospital staff, I did come out of it perfectly healthy. Certainly, the event should prove of interest in elucidating the full usage and treatment options for ECT and deep-brain stimulation.

I believe my concepts in *The Lindemann Theory* on breaking the brain lock of OCD, and then substituting *InfinitE/IQ* to optimize body and brain as a replacement for the breaking mechanism to be unique. I believe one day that ECT may be configured to replace medications as the breaking mechanism – this to avoid the complexity of medications on neurochemistry and the time delay in finding an effective drug.

With this noted, I am an advocate for using medications to break the lock, while beginning *InfinitE/IQ* for the patient. Then I support the gradual, well-supervised withdrawing of medications.

A long time overdo, it is time to investigate the missing components of *InfinitE/IQ* during my adolescence and the years leading to it. I was fifteen years old when the storm hit, and hit hard. The powerful system of *InfinitE/IQ* requires Stimulation, Community and Clean Fuel. It is a formula to maximize life. The stimulation of body and mind was met with educational challenges, Boy Scouts, music lessons, church teachings, sports and hobby activities. Community needs were met by family, friends, teachers, neighbors and church activities. Clean fuel requirements were not met. It is a failure in education that now transcends into the twenty-first century, and a failure whose navigation is confounded by outside influences.

Let's examine my diet for the first fifteen years of my life, and right before the onset of OCD. There was no high-dose EPA or DHA in my diet. I was a pretty active person who ate large quantities of the following: fatty cuts of meats and few fruits. All the vegetables I ate were creamed, candied with brown sugar, laden with cheese, or filled with butter, sour cream and gravies. I ate instant breakfasts, cheese omelets, frozen waffles, pancakes, waffles, English muffins, bleached white-bread toast, cold cuts, mayonnaise, trans-fat oils, "steak" sandwiches, frozen pizza, hotdogs, sausage, cookies, cakes, pies, dips, chips and very little fish. It was offered, but I did not it enjoy at the time. I drank gallons upon gallons of whole milk. Understand, the whole was the problem; 1% milk is fine and good. Whole milk is high in saturated fat; the 1% makes a huge difference.

The school cafeteria took a dive as well, as we all entered high school. Somehow the many food offerings we had in prior grades became fairly limited, and I lived on French fries and oily burgers with fried onions during high school lunches. The biochemical storm was under way, as I awaited the massive hormonal and neurotransmitters changes of adolescence.

We know during puberty a remodeling of the brain occurs,

marked by cerebral cortex neuron and synapse expansion, and what is termed a pruning throughout puberty. More than forty percent of synapses are lost, many in the frontal lobes. The myelin or insulation of the brain expands that results in precision of communication is completed in one's early 20s. The connection between the prefrontal cortex and the midbrain is undergoing major adjustments. Meanwhile, the brain in puberty releases larger quantities of growth hormone, stress hormones and sex hormones. As a male, testosterone increases by a factor of ten, which is significant because sex hormones play major role in the raphe nucleus and limbic system, both a source of the neurotransmitter serotonin. And then we have the hippocampus, which is vulnerable to stress by the aforementioned toxicity of cortisol.

And so, the origin of the illness may have causation effects created by unclean fuels, as well as an unbalanced biochemical and neurotransmitter foundation. The vulnerable foundation is further hampered by major hormonal, brain and body physiological changes, and neurotransmitter changes. The stress of the changes and the age perhaps leaves the hippocampus and other areas of the brain at risk. And so perhaps, the tenuous hormonal and neurotransmitter balance was exposed and unprepared for a very simple eye exam. The change that ensued in my brain became relevant. The result was thirty-one years of hardship. The reversal, cure and an understanding of it became paramount. It became paramount for me, because in good conscience, I found it necessary to share with you.

In 2007, I fell in love. In 2008, I was married. In 2009, assisted by love and community, clean fuel, exercise, DHA/EPA and diligence, I one day I took a run along the Delaware and Raritan Canal Towpath and suddenly stopped in my tracks. I gazed across the water and had an epiphany. I mumbled, "What if?" The what if turned into a self-created historical analysis of my illness, which would lead into *The Lindemann Theory*. The theory turned into action, and then a book, and taking a chance on my fellow man. In 2009, I cured myself of OCD, and have remained symptom, and long-term psychotropic medication and long-term therapy-free since that time.

After five years of symptom-free health, I picked up the phone and asked my medical school to be re-admitted. I hoped for a chance to pass Boards Part I, and to continue my medical education to help others. I left the medical school in good standing for very good reasons; reasons of major medical relevance. I deserve the chance to take a test, a test to lead me further toward helping mankind. They said no. I fought for thirty-one years, I'm prepared for another fight.

And so, this text becomes not just my quest for truth, and not just my quest to prevent others enduring the pain I had. It becomes a journey to justice and dreams, and to help my fellow man.

In 2009, I was reborn. I was rescued. I will allow the love, smiles and warmth from my wife Rosanne, daughters Rhaena and Rochelle and my community to drive me to the finish line. Let me further summate the historical evidence for *The Lindemann Theory*, and expand on *InfinitE/IQ* in the pages to come.

It has been such a pleasure so far, please read further and allow a bit of brain long-term potentiation to lead you to a new and healthy world.

There is nothing wrong, but everything right with hope!

CHAPTER 34

WHAT IF? A RETROSPECTIVE MEDICAL ANALYSIS FOR THE LINDEMANN THEORY

Good morning, all. May the Truth of '2017 set us free! May it be your best day ever!

The path, eight feet in breadth, had a newly-packed, fine granulated base for my lunchtime run. I was heading east from the Bound Brook area towards the town of Bridgewater, New Jersey. As I ran, I looked north towards the Raritan River, in search of the blue heron that typically stands four-foot tall on the northern bank. He was not there on this day. A bit further up the path, I gazed south to the canal side, and found him on the southern canal shore in an attempted camouflage about a fallen tree. It was an unsuccessful effort on this day for this beautiful specimen. I ran further and startled the beauty. He flew, wings extended to a six-foot span, and majestically headed east—directly opposite and past me—and centered to the forty-five-foot width of the canal. It was magical.

When my father past away in July of 2009, a neighbor across from my mother explained her religion's teachings of reincarnation and rebirth. After my father's passing, my mother experienced a rare spotting of a white heron or egret, which actually approached her in an eerie way. She said she knew it was dad.

I wonder now if that magical wing span had meaning, because

it was when I stopped that blue heron on the path that day that I wondered, "What if?" It would be a rebirth for me and a moment of serendipity on this day and path. And yet, by no means a seren- dipitous event was this thirty-one-year ordeal as my parents and I searched and roamed for a solution for three decades. The overall costs were inestimable. It was only when the aspects of *InfinitE/IQ* were in place, my mind was finally free to think for itself. The con- fidence, knowledge, biochemistry and neurochemical changes and history in place, to say, "Let me figure this out myself."

And so, when I came to halt that day, the sweat percolating off my brow, I reflected. The epiphany simply magical and I softly mouthed, "What if?" I knew it to be true.

In the background to this concept of *The Lindemann Theory*, I had the basic analogy of the effects of the drug caffeine. I'll mention several aspects of this drug, again mentioned in a prior chapter. Re- call, it is a member of the xanthine family, a group of central nervous system stimulants. These drugs can be administered orally or rec- tally. So yes, I am forced to ponder the business model, profitability, legality and logistics of a drive-through rectal java shop—an RJS—if you will. But perhaps it is more prudent to reserve the concept for a later writing. Certainly, it's a sign of "maturity" and professionalism to omit this latest epiphanous concept, but unfortunately—and now fortunately—laughter is a major part of *InfinitE/IQ's* components: a merging of community and stimulation.

With the RJS cemented in my readers mind, let us move on. No, no one has validated scientifically that a good chuckle flushes dopa- mine into the brain. Then again, no one has validated the neurologi- cal fireworks release, a 400-foot roping of a baseball creates either. Throw me a couple of million, and Hannibal and I will do the study. Take it from me, folks, when you see life as I do now, the trite of the unappreciative and apathetic becomes the drive for progress, suste-nance, the moment, education, joy and sharing.

Let me share further the caffeine analogy. I have heard many people speak of the need for a coffee boost, as I have heard many speak of the effect of a coffee crash. And I believe we all have heard an individual shout with a bit of overexcitement that they had a little bit too much coffee. Understand, research shows methylxanthines can actually drive one to delirium. Here we have a simple example of a drug creating an upper effect. The human body's normal status quo mechanisms are being overridden, and then suffer a subsequent crash from an exogenous substance. We have the notion this drug might create a little bit of an over-effect, and the self- recognition of it. Ask yourself, if one is flying high on four cups of coffee and the numbers 8, 17, 45, 60, and 64 with a Powerball of 4 and Megaplier of 3X, might not the cuckoo's nest be a possibility, when the $500 mil-lion check is flashed in your face?

I understand that not all the mood boosters I was given during this thirty-one-year ordeal were <u>direct</u> central nervous stimulants. All were though, in design and patent, formulated to boost mood and neurotransmitter levels. Mechanism of action varied, of course. In effect, I think it is fair to say it was possible this same type of phe-nomenon could occur with mood enhancers that were creating long-term receptor changes in the human brain, as well as other effects. Understand as well, we are talking about a more, powerful direct ef-fect on the brain. There's one of constancy, as daily regimented doses of medications are given.

Let's expand on this simple analogy, and cover the plausibility of one drug's effects leading to another being prescribed without understanding the root cause: that is the original drug. It has been mentioned previously, the very length and unpredictability of the clearance from the body of caffeine is complicated by its metabolite being an actual drug in itself: a pro-drug.

An individual who drinks caffeine and suffers insomnia on a regular basis, one unaware of the clearance or power of caffeine, might choose to pursue a sleep medication. So, we have a case where one drug leads to another. Now, it is very well known, many sleep aids do not allow humans to reach deep, restorative sleep. Therefore, the brain myelin is never fully manufactured at night, and the individual suffers at work the next day. Now, this occurs on the second day. The human fears lack of efficiency at work, and doubles down on the coffee to offset his lacking brain insulation, and the cycle becomes apparent. One cup turns to two, then three. With this cycle, the upper boost and eventual crash effect can only magnify and become more dramatic.

Let's take this a step further, and see how the cycle can affect other body systems, as the drug dose begins to increase and becomes more regular. It should be noted at this time, caffeine can also lead to acid reflux: causation being the relaxation and weakening of the lower esophageal sphincter. Someone with acid reflux might begin to take antacids. An uncontrolled acid reflux can make changes to the esophageal lining, and the result could be an adenocarcinoma (cancer of the esophagus). Unfortunately, adenocarcinoma of the distal esophagus, when discovered—is usually far advanced. It's relatively unresponsive to radiation therapy or chemotherapy. Do you think the above scenario happens often? Education is so important. A healthcare system that does not promote haste for our physicians becomes paramount! They need time, and to be paid for time to diagnose patients.

So, we have an exogenous substance entering the body and disrupting five million years of balance. The substance has been shown to cause an up and down effect, create sequelae, draw in new medications and advance damage to other body systems. No, not all exogenous substances are harmful. The aforementioned EPA AND DHA are extremely beneficial. For accuracy, EPA and DHA are manufactured within the human body, though not as efficiently as desired. They are not truly exogenous, but the point remains.

With this background in place, let us head back to the Towpath Trail, and enter my brain's memories from thirty-one years. Let me first summate this ordeal with a vivid review of clinical historical data, so you are certain why I have written this material and you do not have to experience the ordeal I did. It is said the Buddha went through extreme personal deprivation to seek enlightenment. If you so desire to avoid sex and wander in a desert, eating scorpions and sucking cacti dry to understand pain and suffering—all the power to you. My goal is for you to avoid the deprivation, and use education and insight to find the light. Please understand the dramatic effect *InfinitE/IQ* could have on health-care costs. While the analysis may be technical, I can only ask you to examine it carefully, for maximum understanding.

Below is a list to pay attention to. I hope to never write it again.

Thirty-one Years – A Summation of my Clinical History:

* scale of one to ten for pain, discomfort, anxiety

Total Number of Doctor Visits (typically one hour) = in the 1,000s (fifty-two weeks and thirty-one years)

Total Number of Direct Different Doctors = 12

Total Number of Doctors Direct and Indirect = 100s

Number of Different Medications = Near 20

Number of Unsuccessful Therapies, Pre-OCD Experimental

Drug = <u>8</u>

Number of Major Hospitalizations (One Week Or Longer) = <u>6</u>

Number of Sleep Research Facilities Tested On = <u>1</u>

Number of Lock Downs = <u>2</u>

Number of Different Depressive Events Requiring ECT = <u>3</u>

Number of E.R. Visits Because of Illness= <u>5</u>

Total Major Depression Periods = <u>4</u>

Total Hallucination Events Including Full Psychosis = 2

Total Burnouts = <u>10 - 15</u>

Total Different Long-Term Obsessional Periods = <u>3</u>

Pain (Mental) Level of OCD = <u>15</u> (Anxiety Level: <u>10</u>; Stress Level: <u>10</u>; Physical Pain: <u>0</u>)
Physical Exhaustion: <u>9</u>

Pain Level of Major Depression = <u>10</u> (Anxiety Level: <u>1</u>; Physical Pain: <u>7 - 8</u>; Mental Pain: Seven; Physical Exhaustion: <u>20</u>)

Pain Level of Hallucinations = <u>0</u> (Anxiety, Fear <u>2</u>)

Pain Level of Paranoia = <u>2</u> (Anxiety <u>5</u>)

Total Cost In Dollars = ?

Total Stress and Effect On Family Members = ?

Okay, that was difficult. I hope the above data pushes you to consider my conclusion and recommendations. At bear minimum, to begin a discussion. Let us move to my retrospective analysis of my case history.

<u>31 Year Medical Case Analysis</u>

1) In July of 1978, Robert Wesley Lindemann's brain pathology is one of brain-lock: an unrelenting, nonstop case of OCD with symptoms of non-existent conflicts and ritual compulsions to unsuccessfully resolve. One conflict is resolved, only to be substituted by one with more power. Obsessions often disrupted or extended into sleep, though not fully. Results were extreme mental pain, stress and anxiety, starving the physical as well, with obvious difficulty in focused concentration.

Possible causation of the brain-lock attributed to the hormonal, neurotransmitter, physical storm changes of adolescence, combined with an unclean fueling system, creating aberrant physiology.

2) In August of 1981, he matriculated at a university in North Carolina, and experienced a four to six-week period of total elimination of OCD symptoms. Stress and anxiety were removed and focus returned.

Today, he theorizes with personal certainty, an environmental and life event acted as a mood booster of dopamine, norepinephrine and serotonin. He was able to boost neurotransmitter levels to a healthy state, above a safe and normal balance line. The rapidity at which it happened indicates the state of OCD endured for three years, but did not create permanent receptor or permanent physiological changes. Again, this was not a gradual reduction of symptoms, rather an all-or-none scenario: the latter a pattern descriptive of relief throughout this ordeal.

It is apparent to the author the stress and anxiety of OCD is created by the belief the obsessions and thoughts are real for the patient, no matter how absurd for the clinician or world. This brings into doubt the use of anxiolytics by clinicians for the treatment of OCD.

Anxiolytics are not intended to remove obsessions, which are the source of the stress and anxiety. They cannot have an effect on reducing anxiety: the obsessions are the source. Anxiolytics will confound and confuse the patient's biochemistry, further creating an environment whereby the OCD drugs may not work, or worse—create more sequelae. Again, this would be a tragic mistake.

The return of OCD after four to six weeks ensued after the natural high was gone, and natural stresses came in. Unclean fueling continued, which indicates cortisol may have begun its toxic hippocampal-neuron effects, bringing Robert's healthy, slow simmer of neurotransmitters to a flat, below balance line: resulting in the return of OCD pathology.

Departure from college was a life event that drew in depressive pathology as well. The re-entrance of symptoms, after their departure, was both scary and heart-ripping for the patient.

3) The successful introduction of an experimental drug in March of 1982 and its action—receptor modification in the cerebral cortex and hippocampus—resulted in increased noradrenaline and serotonin. It began his understanding of brain geography and chemistry involvement. The drug was a tricyclic antidepressant.

The success of the drug indicates an exogenous substance can be used to remove all OCD symptoms, and these two neurotransmitters (or at least one) are involved in the causation of the illness. This drug boosted mood and took levels to a safe baseline, and/or above normal brain chemistry.

The drug left the patient with the inability to orgasm: a human function known to release dopamine and provide natural anxiolytic action. A medication of equal efficacy and void of this side effect, and with no other more detrimental side effects, would be more preferable.

Of most importance, in pre-market testing of this drug, it was noted hypomania and mania were seen in several patients, as well as the following: delusions, hallucinations, psychotic episodes, confusion and paranoia. The patient was unaware of this until 2017. It becomes an easy extrapolation to understand the possibility mood boosters can overly boost. In thirty-one years of treatment this notion was never bought to Robert's attention. It became obvious to him on the running path that day, but now we see evidence very far back in time. The latter discovery is concerning.

4) In the summer of 1983, Robert experienced his first of many burnouts from mood boosters: this one caused by the experimental drug. In *The Lindemann Theory*, he proposes mood boosters can allow one to override the natural control mechanisms of the adrenal-cortisol-brain axis. If one has a Type-A personality, this might leave the drug and cortisol at an even more vulnerable position. Unlike the other drug, which caused burnouts of four to six weeks, this medication actually stopped working all together. No conclusion of cessation of action could be reached.

So, we have a situation where a delicate balance of brain chemistry needs to be respected. We have the notion mood boosters may allow one to override natural protection mechanisms, and the need for patient education on this matter. We also have the need to understand personality types when such medications are taken. A means to monitor adrenal health—an obvious goal—while taking such medications, as well as the monitoring of brain chemistry levels. The latter, of course, is expensive.

5) In 1983 and 1984, Robert was given a drug combination for OCD that was successful. It involved a monoamine-oxidase inhibitor and a tricyclic antidepressant. Both drugs increase norepinephrine and serotonin levels. It was noted, at the time of

this writing, this combination has the warning of Serotonin Syndrome, which includes the warning of hallucinations as a side effect. Robert would go on to experience burnouts, delusions and a hallucinatory event with this combination. The events were never attributed to the drug. Robert could not orgasm, or it was very difficult on this drug combination.

We have further evidence elevating norepinephrine and serotonin can eliminate OCD. We have further evidence these drugs can lead to burnouts and mania-type symptoms.

6) In September of 1990, Robert had a hallucination and psychotic break while at medical school, causing him to withdraw. In a retrospective review, an off-euphoria sensation existed, leading up to the entrance to medical school. Robert theorized the combination of the medication boost with the natural life high event propelled him into mania, hallucinations and psychosis.

7) In 1990 and 1991, Robert would need a dopamine booster with action on norepinephrine to allow him to escape a depression. While eliminating the depression, it took away his OCD as well. It did so without boosting serotonin.

So, we have evidence of another neurotransmitter possibly involved with OCD: dopamine. Robert would have burnout and mania with this drug also. This drug had the advantage of allowing Robert to orgasm. This is significant because the human orgasm can be very health beneficial, as a stress and anxiety reducer and mood elevator. Known increases in dopamine, oxytocin, prolactin and androgen receptors can occur. With stress reduction always a part of any wellness program, elimination of the inability to orgasm was significant. Allowance of the neurochemistry of sex, as an adjunct, was much welcomed.

8) From February of 2002 to July of 2002, Robert researched and embraced clean-food fuel, allowing him to shed sixty-five pounds and realign his blood chemistry panel. Rigorous exercise enhanced the mood-boosting effect. Feeling better, Robert actually felt too good, with the same off-euphoric feeling he'd experienced while entering medical school. Robert added high doses of EPA and DHA. The biochemical advantages of clean fuel were discussed. Robert would go on to have a psychotic break.

Robert observed a drug-mood booster, plus a clean-fuel program and exercise could have additive effects and lead to mania.

And so, that day on the path, I looked back at this history of eight items and said, "What if?" I went home that night and sat at my office desk, and the following epiphany occurred. I said, "What if?"

What if an adolescent sub-normal level of neurotransmitter levels existed because of adolescent brain maturation changes, and an unclean fuel program. The combination resulted in brain-lock: OCD pathology. This shows significance, in that unclean fuel could have a negative impact on brain chemistry, making clean fuel a possibility of major positive benefit for brain health, specific to the disorder, origin and causation.

I knew a mood-boosting life event could be significant in raising neurotransmitters. I knew that clean fuel boosted mood, as did EPA AND DHA and my intense exercise program. Now when Medication + Clean Fuel + EPA AND DHA + Exercise + Type A to drive mood was all added, the result was over-mood stimulation and mania.

If the medication were eliminated, could all the components of

InfinitE/IQ (stimulation, community and clean fuel) sustain and allow thriving of brain health? In turn, could I eliminate the exogenous substance known by me to create burnouts, and in combination with some of the components, induce an overly heightened mood and mania?

I could naturally re-enter our five million years of evolution, work the balance naturally and live the cure.

I approached Dr. Rull in 2009 with the idea, and he understandably said he could not take me off the dopamine/NE enhancer in good conscience. I had no choice but to wean myself off the medication. The result has been remarkable.

For the last nine plus years, I have experienced zero OCD symptoms, zero burnouts and zero hallucinations. I have never felt better—literally like I felt when I was fifteen years old, before it started. I have also felt the following return: creative, complex and confident thinking, drive and ambition, and a thirst to learn.

I believe these ideas have worldwide health applications and implications. In the next chapter, I will expand further on the details of *InfinitE/IQ* and offer further insight into OCD, other mental disorders and a means to healthier more joyous living.

Stimulation (mental and physical challenges) that we adapt and progress to, community, love, beliefs, family, sex, friendships, sharing, giving and becoming the social creature we are, along with clean fuel: protein, carbohydrates and fat—together—of the right type and combination to maximize the human machine, and EPA AND DHA to enhance biochemistry and neurochemical streams become the formula: the triad of *InfinitE/IQ* .

Enjoy the next chapter, as an invitation to a happier existence. Embrace our past evolution, treat the mind and body as a whole and let us progress forward on this planet as one.

Open your heart, and let your emotions paint the pages with words of passion, inspiration and knowledge!

CHAPTER 35

RECOMMENDATIONS, PROGRESS AND THE ADVANCEMENT OF InfinitE/IQ – PART I

Thank you so much, my reader. I have poured my heart out to the world, some seven-plus billion human beings, and if only one of you has chosen to read, listen and heed my words, I so thank you! Whatever happens to these words, always remember one thing my reader, there is nothing, nothing—absolutely nothing—wrong, but everything right with hope, faith and the diligence to examine truth and share it with others. A work ethic, faith, and the ability to question and solve and control man's greatest gift and detriment— one's ego—is what will lead us forward in progress.

Mr. Henley and Kortchmar penned out over five minutes of lyrics and rhythm in "Dirty Laundry", the first track in *Actual Miles: Henley's Greatest Hits*. The message, from my viewpoint, is to say: let us move forward, let us survive and solve the world's problems with intelligence—not ego—or self or group-driven quandaries. Let us release the preoccupation with the irrelevant and mundane. The purpose of history is to exam, research, settle injustice and then advance out of mistakes made—not to dwell and confuse the advancement. These points, my friends, I believe to be <u>not</u> simply a matter of philosophy, politics or choice, but of urgency and survival of our species.

Today in New Jersey at 1:30 p.m., we will be having a total solar eclipse. The moon's apparent diameter becomes larger than that of the sun, a fascinating perhaps serendipitous event for me, as the last solar eclipse was in 1979, my illness still in its infancy.

Today, I will be finishing up the last two chapters of this book for you, with tomorrow's light bringing my final conclusions. I remember the filtering glasses back in 1979, the retina, unequipped with pain feedback sensors—the recommendation a good one, to give attention to a valid fear. And so, they have calculated a 700-million-dollar loss today in productivity for the USA as we search for an eclipse. Perhaps the event will stimulate enough BDNF and sense of community to exceed our goals by the end of week.

The excitement within me right now, to conclude this writing with final recommendations, and expand on *InfinitE/IQ*, leaves me filled with joy. My fingers feel light and nimble, my mind feels unparalleled lucidness, my heart pounds with pride and I feel a hopeful light will be shed from this memoir. I seem unphased and fearless of detractors. I simply feel with watery eyes, the warmth and hearts of seven billion comrades. I feel free. I really feel free. Thirty-one fucking years, I feel so free!

It is necessary, before furthering this discussion, to remind the reader I am not a medical doctor. No recommendations below should be embraced without review by a physician. With this said, I have an immense academic education in psychology, all aspects of the human body, and medicine, as well as thirty-one clinical years of real-world experience in the field of psychology, pharmacology and physiology. I have experienced the symptoms of obsessive-compulsive disorder, depression and suicidal ideation. I have also experienced, via my proposed medicine-induced sequelae or side effects, the symptoms of burnout, delusions, hallucinations, psychosis and paranoia, and have almost experienced a panic attack. Due to these these created

THE LINDEMANN THEORY • 225

sequelae, I believe I have an insight into manic-depressive disorder, cyclothymic disorder, schizophrenia, panic attacks, anorexia, bulimia, body dysmorphic disorder and anxiety disorders.

As you know from a previous chapter, I felt compelled to redefine the definition of OCD, the reason being, many individuals I have spoken with have confused anxiety disorders with OCD. By no means does this lessen the severity of anxiety disorders. My concern, from my experience, is the mental pain and anguish of OCD is so severe, it is dangerous to proceed with therapies that do not involve medications to break the cycle—and break it fast.

Is it possible a less severe and treatable behavioral form of OCD exists? I don't know. Again, the level of pain I endured with the OCD brings the concern of suicide to light. It is this concern with suicide that warrants urgency for the OCD patient. It is also my knowledge of suicidal ideation that warrants urgency. An individual pondering suicide is unaware of how powerful and rapid the beast can engage and swallow one whole. As a clinician, make sure you get by any means possible a truthful answer to the question,

"Are you suicidal?"

Understand, as I did not in my first suicide attempt, when the final yearn to end one's life comes, it comes fast—and you are without defense. Educating one on suicide does not propagate suicide, or ideas of or for it. Suicide, attempted suicide or suicidal ideation is not a sin. It is by no means a cowardice state. It is a biochemical and medical travesty, thrusting an organism in despair to enter what they most fear: death. I imagine a family being told their child was a coward for committing suicide, and I become nauseated at the ignorance, arrogance and the filth of ego that abounds. You want entrance to the fiery inferno of hell, go ahead and make that comment!

Now, I have incorporated *InfinitE/IQ* as a cure for OCD, post breaking the lock, and a means to achieve optimal brain and body health. The question, of course, should be why not simply apply and utilize *InfinitE/IQ* when OCD begins in a patient—or any psychiatric disorder? My answer, of course, is absolutely do so and with hope, and I will expand on this in a bit. My concern: with my formula being curative while a patient is in full-blown OCD and full-blown bed-ridden depression, is the following.

Remember, in full-blown OCD, the patient's level of stress and anxiety is so severe, cortisol production is killing neurons in the hip-pocampus. My concern is the biochemical changes via *InfinitE/IQ* will be unable to keep pace with the stress, anxiety and destructive cortisol production of the OCD disorder itself. The same argument would hold for full-blown depression. So while I encourage my triad as a treatment and eventual cure, my argument is one of safety: sui-cide concerns. First, we must break the cycle of OCD and the abyss of full-blown depression with medications, and/or ECT and deep brain stimulation. In my thirty-one-year ordeal, I found four medications (one of which was a combination) that totally alleviated all symp-toms of OCD. One of the medications that was taken was needed when there was a breakthrough of obsessions through another (the dopamine agonist/reuptake inhibitor). Those four medications in-cluded a TCA, a combination of an MAOI with a TCA, a dopamine agonist (reuptake inhibitor) with NE properties and a SSRI. The SSRI was not taken for long, so there will be no discussion of created burn-outs or mania with this drug: it was also taken with the dopamine/NE medication. When I took the first TCA, I experienced burnouts, but no mania (again I did not take that long: one year). This medi-cation inexplicably stopped working. The MAOI and TCA combi-nation produced burnouts and mania, as did the dopamine agonist with NE effects. The dopamine agonist is the only drug that allowed for the ability to orgasm with ease.

With that said, per the dopamine agonist, the dopamine reuptake inhibitor/NE effects do stimulate the central nervous system (CNS). With this said, I would like to raise a question. It is known that the CNS depressants, such as alcohol, depress inhibitory pathways in the CNS. If the dopamine reuptake inhibitor were to increase CNS activity, would it be fair to say the drug would increase inhibition? From my experience, I know being inhibited can be a precursor to paranoia. Thus, is it fair to say the paranoia I did experience at times with this drug was attributed to direct CNS activation? I do not believe any of the drugs directly contributed to suicidal ideation: the latter the result of real life and pain. With this noted, the side effects created by the medications created the environment that would lead me to suicidal ideation. Indirectly those medications did lead me to suicidal ideation and an attempt, in my opinion.

One last final note, and with it noted I have a very good education on drug clearance and excretion systems: If you are a patient with mental illness, you have to be sure you are not taking any alcohol/un-prescribed drugs, with your prescription medication. These exogenous drugs can really confound, compete with or activate the very systems that metabolize the medications you are taking. In summary, they really confuse everything—don't do it.

Again, chronic alcohol ingestion will increase the liver monoxygenase enzymes and the cytochrome P450 system, and accelerate your medication clearance from the body. You will not have enough medication in your system, and you won't know it. If you acutely abuse alcohol (one major all-nighter) you can actually intensify medication effects by inhibiting drug metabolism. Becoming well and healthy requires responsibility and education, and knowledge that these not prescribed, exogenous substances perceived palliative effects will be the death to you.

So, I am recommending to the clinician to be aware of the ups and downs of the mood-booster medicated patient. If outfitted with *InfinitE/IQ*. The goal, of course, is to lift the OCD. It will lift the depression with medication and utilize the Triad to invoke a natural cure by replacing the drugs, and maximize life performance.

Why am I concerned about the medications? Again, the balance of biochemistry and neurochemistry is a delicate one, and filled with many feedback mechanisms. Actually, delicate is the wrong word! The balance is a natural one. The hormonal and neurochemical communication is filled with so many interactions and feedback mechanisms. It is actually a strong balance, but an exogenous substance can create absolute communication chaos. Unclean fuel can have the very same effect. For thirty-one years, once rid of OCD, the inability of the medications to adapt to my milieu, left a protracted and chaotic path: one again, I long for you to avoid.

The wonderful news is that if you are predisposed to either OCD or clinical depression, my System can be your preventive fix. Without a doubt, the pre-OCD patient most likely was an individual who worried more than normal, and the pre-clinically depressed patient suffered malaise, sadness and anxiety prior to a bedridden state. It is in this pre-condition where I am convinced *InfinitE/IQ* can possibly eliminate the need for medicine, of course preventing the onset of illness. I believe this to be true for full-blown anxiety disorders as well.

Nip it in the bud, would define the action of *InfinitE/IQ*. Psychotherapy and behavioral therapies might be a perfect fit, along with the powerful three of Clean Fuel, Stimulation and Community for some disorders. For me, and as someone who experienced all I did, I never needed psychotherapy. Actually, the only time a needed therapy was after my cure—an LOL I will perhaps describe in a separate writing.

You may recall, I made mention of the component of fear in my discussion on OCD, and when I almost suffered an anxiety attack. By the way, it was my prior experience with mental illness which allowed me to recognize the on-coming anxiety attack. This discussion of fear in mental illness is very important from a cognitive-behavioral approach to these disorders. For OCD, can an understanding of fear break the cycle? I don't think so, but I would surely introduce it as an option. For panic attacks, I am convinced this understanding can help the panic attack victim. Let's explore a bit.

When I suffered my first obsession in 1978, the fear of lost control of rational thought was an immediate adjunct to the obsessions themselves. On the earth for fifteen years, with no awareness of the power of the mind, I was suddenly thrust into the inability to control a thought. It was a fearful event. The clinician needs to explain this to a patient. I believe our educational system should tackle early on some of these basic natural psychological phenomena: fear, ego and coveting. I believe the fear I experienced upon the first obsession helped perpetuate the cycle, much like an error-laden infielder. You can suffer a loss of confidence.

When I was in that off-euphoric" state I have described in this memoir, I recognized the state as aberrant. The generated fear would exasperate the state towards falling off the shelf—full psychosis—

feeling. And with the near-anxiety attack I experienced, I could immediately perceive if an individual had one attack. The fear of the next would create a self-fulfilling prophecy. You might as well assign a mental confidence, or lost mental confidence, in this discussion. The clinician needs to come and say, "Hey, this is what happened on that anxiety attack. It is OK to be afraid, but if you recognize the fear and become aware of it, and can comprehend the statement 'there is nothing to fear but fear itself', then you are well on your way, Take a seat, perform some deep breathing and seek potential control."

And so, we are lead to that discussion of fear. Fear is ours to control. Fear creates worry. Use fear and worry to your advantage, and comprehend it is not an uncontrollable entity, but rather grab it, recognize it, control it and use it. Worry becomes a useless waste of energy when uncontrolled. Once again, I will use the example of an upcoming test. If the worry propels you forward to study, use it to do so. When the test comes, whether prepared or not, worry will only hamper performance. An anxious mind is a frozen mind, in memory and rational. Worrying the baseball hurler just hit ninety-five MPH on the radar gun will not help you hit the ball: it will do exactly the opposite. Eyes and hands detest worry, and love embracing the speed concept. The bulk of a sports psychologist's task is to harness his patients understanding and approach to fear.

With above noted, respect fear as well: again, use it to advantage, as it has purpose. A motorcyclist, who hits a pothole at sixty-five MPH and is tossed onto asphalt, requires fear to drive them to be even more observant of a path's hidden danger.

In my discussion of my illness, I did show dismay. In thirty-one years, the concept of medication-induced mania or burnout, nor the concept of reducing medication dosages, were never discussed. Please understand, these medications do require a therapeutic range where they exert their effect, in the case of the drugs I was taking for OCD. I believe most, if not all, require long-term receptor changes. But I believe the drugs also initiate initial and immediate changes, but not long-term changes. Also recall, the amount needed to break the cycle, competing with the toxic effects of cortisol, might be greater than needed to sustain health and avoid predisposing patients to burnouts or mania. So again, with no time to research now and an urgency to message all, I reserve the question of backing off a bit on medications once the cycle is broken to be open to future investigation.

I would like to make one final note as matter of awareness regarding pharmacokinetics, a fascinating science, which is the study of the movement of drugs throughout body systems. A Swedish study was completed on genetic-clearance variations on the drug nortriptyline. This drug is a TCA, the same class as my experimental drug, and the drug combined with my MAOI drug. The study showed a 100-fold difference in plasma half-life of this agent in a large group of patients. As a very important note: rapid metabolizers might experience undermedicated effects—or none at all—while slower metabolizers might experience toxic effects. Perhaps with better access to genetic analysis, clinicians may utilize this knowledge in prescribing medications.

The Lindemann Theory understands the brain-lock of OCD to be created by real long-term stress and anxiety that maintains cortisol levels at high levels, toxic to hippocampal neurons. Thus, a self-fulfilling loop of agony is created. While hopeful *InfinitE/IQ* induced physiological changes and discussions of fear might abate the obsessions, concern for the safety with suicidal ideation leads me to suggest immediate medications. The use of anxiolytics seems senseless and can confound the desired biochemical changes, deemed senseless as they do not target the origin of the anxiety: the obsessions.

The theory goes on to understand burnout to represent the medication-induced overriding of the adrenal-cortisol-brain axis. The concept of personality types to help in this override was examined, and should be examined by the clinician. The Type-A personality is more apt to push beyond a medication mood boost that really burns the chemistry. My theory went on to describe a simmering pot of water, where during life-ecstatic events and clean fuel, the balance can be tipped high, resulting in mania, delusions, hallucinations and psychosis. The burnout and mania can be misdiagnosed and draw in new medications. For me, the burnouts were misdiagnosed as bipolar illness drawing in a medication, causing nephrogenic diabetes insipidus over time (permanent, yet non-progressive, kidney damage). The created mania drew in prescribed drugs that acted as major tranquilizers. I also was prescribed anxiolytics to no avail, furthering the biochemical storm.

The other important manifestation of a misdiagnosis is the clinician who moved away from solving the origin of the problem in the first place. In my case, the medications created confusion. Nine plus years of clinical evidence in my cure should suffice to support this in my opinion.

This further examination of my case history sets the stage for the concluding chapter, Part II and an elaboration of *InfinitE/IQ*. Enjoy this final chapter, as the concepts can prevent illness, treat illness and lead to longevity, happiness and hope.

There is nothing wrong, but everything right with hope!

CHAPTER 36

RECOMMENDATIONS, PROGRESS, THE ADVANCEMENT OF InfinitE/IQ – PART II

What a beautiful day! It's the finish line, but I hope a finish that will lead to further discussions, questions and solutions for all. The case analysis has led us to simply further and summate details of *InfinitE/IQ*, and afford me one last chance to say thank you.

Let me provide a solution. *The Lindemann Theory* calls for slow medication withdrawal after brain-lock cessation, while having already implemented the tools of my Triad: Stimulation, Community and Clean Fuel. Let us examine these three in review and expanded versions, and welcome health on every physiological, psychological and societal level. Please be cognizant in review of these three, and the major healthcare savings to be seen if we all take on my Formula in our lives and education. And please, understand the personal responsibility implicit for healthcare expansion.

InfinitE/IQ's stimulation encompasses challenges to our physical, mental and spiritual entities, to bring about adaptive changes for health and the enjoyment of life. Physically, our goals are to improve cardiovascular capabilities, hormonal and fuel control, and to recruit dormant stem cells to lay desired sliding filaments and inspire angiogenesis and nouveaux nerve innervation. Mentally, we are looking to expand the wonders of the brain, let dendrites expand and fire with wonderfully bathed synapses and optimally fueled neurons, and communicate in harmony to reason, analyze and to solve. Spiritually, we are searching and searching and searching, but we should seek solidity with convictions and principals of faith, hope, love and harmony. Let the golden rule, rule.

Let us delve a bit further into how stimulating the human body can benefit us all. The extraordinary health benefits of exercise have been well-documented. The anti-aging effects on the human body have been more difficult to quantify. Yet, it is this author's opinion it is a big yes in the delay of onset of chronic disease, a reduction in injuries and an improved quality of life. Would you not agree: a trained senior is less likely to fall and sustain a broken hip?

Systems improved and effected include cardiovascular, pulmonary, endocrine, neural and more. With an improvement of all systems, we have a milieu of less stress and better function. An endurance-trained athlete can enjoy an increase in muscle glycogen, number of mitochondria (the powerhouse of the cell), mitochondrial volume, resting ATP (the transfer of chemical energy), phosphorylase and succinate dehydrogenase, maximum stroke volume, cardiac output, reduced resting heart rate, Max VO2 and Max O2 diff, heart volume, blood volume and Ve max, as well as a reduced resting heart rate and a reduced percentage of body fat.

On the anaerobic training side (strength), we see major increases of anaerobic substrates (ATP, CP, free creatine and glycogen), major increases in amounts and speed of key enzymes, and increases in fast-twitch fiber size and the capacity to deal with blood lactic acid.

Understand though that chronic or excess exercise, can lead to excess cortisol production, increased caloric expenditure, and possibly have the reverse desired effect on aging. What is incredible is that nerve-conductive velocity is the least effected parameter of physiology as we age. Can that speed ball still be tapped at eighty years of age? Perhaps some of Bruce Springsteen's *Glory Days*, can be within access after all.

You train and you exercise, and your body responds and adapts and performs. Enjoy the effects of your work, with progress—progress that overlap in to all categories of *InfinitE/IQ*.

The following section is a very high-level summary on brain physiology and neurotransmission, and the magnificent effects of exercise on it.

Exercise increases the production of BDNF, a factor required for new neural growth. In taking DHA, a component in clean fuel, you now have the components for new neural growth. BDNF's specific function is to sprout new dendrites between nerves or neurons, these dendrites are the essence of learning. During a lifetime, one neuron can make 20,000 such connections with other neurons. The brain, like the body, adapts to good stress: the body receives exercise, and the brain mentally exercises by reading, studying and thinking. With BDNF release, a bit of mental exercise and DHA from your clean fuel program, feel free to build a lightning-fast, creative brain.

Exercise lowers excess blood glucose and lowers insulin, and helps provide a steady uniform flow of glucose; the brain loves steady glucose. Again, as long as the exercise is not excessive, the above two components ensure cortisol is not excessive. This is extremely important as excess cortisol is toxic and kills neurons and by all means not conducive to the desired dendrite explosion desired, nor optimal brain health.

Please note: the steady constant supply of glucose to the brain is paramount to brain health. Uniform glucose maintains adequate ATP in brain-neuron mitochondria, needed to pump out excitatory neurotransmitters into surrounding glia cells for storage. Not enough glucose can be toxic to neurons. In addition, too much glucose can also be toxic, as neuron glucoreceptors are very sensitive.

And, of course, the brain needs oxygen. As the cardiopulmonary benefits of exercise increases, so does brain health in turn.

It should be noted, eating correctly before and after exercise can greatly magnify all of the effects, as well. Exercise with better efficiency and concentration, recover faster, and develop and adapt faster. Remember, correct training plus clean fuel is self-fulfilling as well, leading to fewer injuries and continued training. Injuries are an athlete's worst nightmare. The reversal of the training effects can be rapid; do not despair, training advancements can be just as rapid.

Of course, exercise can take a variety of forms—and enjoy your exercise. If you have been cleared by a doctor, enjoy the maximum benefits—both mental and physical. Hit it hard a few times per week, while understanding training safety, and avoiding injuries.

It is my opinion our educational system and the workplace need to reembrace the benefits of exercise in building a better student and employee. We can advance this to our healthcare system as well. Develop and reward the physically trained students, employees and insured citizens. A human being does not have to be an athlete to see these rewards. A student who sustains his heart rate above a certain level, or is physically engaged to the point of difficulty for twenty-five minutes, has just enjoyed an aerobic workout. A student who strength trains and feels pain in his muscles forty-eight hours later has accomplished positive work: the body heals and rewards. Work ethic an overriding principal in *InfinitE/IQ* is required of course; the rewards will be tremendous.

Mental challenges will be required to stimulate and build a better brain. The goal, of course, is to have every neuron make those 20,000 connections with every other neuron. We want to stress neurons with reading, problem-solving, creative thinking, innovation, art, theater, music, laughter and more—to sprout new dendrites and advance our faculties. The very basics of the neurobiology of learning encompass four generalizations:

1) Plastic changes, leading to long-term memory, are not located in any one brain region, but rather in multiple areas of the nervous system.

2) Memory has stages: its vision is always changing.

3) Long-term memory does occur via plastic changes in the brain.

4) Reflexive and declarative memories involve different neuronal circuits.

If you want to learn and remember, I'd like to add my own rules:

1) Never re-read material, over and over again.

2) Read, close the text, and write or what you remember. While you write, talk about what you remember, and draw and diagram to draw in other parts and circuits of the brain.

3) Build upon what you have learned, and expand the memories to create long-term potentiation.

4) Ask questions aloud, always engaging the lips and vocal cords to engage the motor cortex, and research the questions.

5) Meet with others and engage in quizzes and questions.

6) Be fearless of study time and test time. Understand the slower path to learning will sustain memories over a lifetime.

7) If you have a problem, do your best to solve it. Then you have it for a lifetime: remember riding a bike!

8) Understand haste makes waste (avoid traditional ideas like, "Just memorize it". Follow the turtle and avoid the rabbit snare, and you will find your relaxed brain remembers.

9) Embrace technology, but do not let it replace and de-evolve you. Build your brain, utilize technology for speed and enjoy the un-squashed apples of your labor.

As with exercise, get over the hump with mental work and enjoy the ride once your systems start to process. Meet urges to procrastinate with visualizations of pride in a completed task, and an understanding your mind and body will ride the wave. BDNF is just waiting to be activated and released—activate a splash. Visualize play after the boxing match!

Spiritual challenges become the final component of stimulation in *InfinitE/IQ*. Be it faith, hope, heart, determination, will, drive and motivation, embrace this human attribute—and let it help you and others. Estimates state there are around twenty major religions, with ideologies in the thousands. The probability of all of them being correct is slim—and the probability of them all being right might be great. Most of the major religions embrace the golden rule, the concept of man helping his fellow man, and the concept of love and the desire not to harm. They embrace the idea there is something beyond man. Atheism holds a faith as well: they believe, they do not believe.

At the beginning of this book, I stated quite frankly I don't have all the answers. I was quick to point out there must be something beyond us, beyond our concept of science. I acknowledge our specie's faults, but retain faith in our attributes. When I sit in church, I do feel a power, a sense of community and peace: a holy spirit. Do I have a tough time trying to understand why I had a thirty-one-year-old struggle? Yes, I do, but I retain the drive to move forward and to love, and certainly a desire to prevent—if possible—others from enduring the pain of my struggle.

Like many of you, I have no idea why I am on this planet. I don't know why I just typed over 50,000 words for an audience I do not know, or have any idea how it will be received. I do feel warmth in my hands and heart, aside from an overheated computer! I do hope these words can fulfill people, teach empathy and help everyone understand that questioning details is paramount. For the narcissist—selfish and manipulative—I also pray, but with understanding and patience on a measured leash. To live in faith by no means negates the need to protect and prosper, if impeded by evil. When I embrace my daughters Rhaena and Rochelle, and hold my wife, I simply feel there is more than any of us know—and that is just fine for me. The embrace of a loved one may indeed be the ultimate answer.

With stimulation summarized, a natural bridge to *InfinitE/IQ*'s community becomes apparent. Community embodies friendships, organizations, family, sex, hobbies, meditation, activities, relaxation, fun, restful sleep and an observation that—as *Homo sapiens*—we are a social creature. Our advanced brain and sense of self also leaves us with a sense of you. Now, if science doesn't explain it, common sense might help out. With 7.5 billion of us, folks, as of 2017 and 11.2 billion by 2100, if might be a good idea for all of us to get along on this rotating four-billion-year-old sphere. Even better, let's advance and prosper, to endure here and beyond. With estimates of solar systems outside our own, sitting between 100 million and 100 billion, perhaps one day there will be another place to hang one's hat.

I have described in this text the deleterious and isolating effects of mental illness: the lonely and emptiness of the abyss witnessed from first-hand experience. I also described two situations at long-term stay facilities where the effect of isolation had a profound effect on me. The reverse was explored, as well, where a nourishing, intentional community would be conducive to getting better, and allowing medications a lessened fight against the stress and cortisol pounding one has on the outside.

Alone, one is left to dwell. Neurotransmitters in a vibrant simmer might flat line, and so the vibrancy of life is further diminished. Of course, let us not forget the extreme difficulty the patient afflicted with mental illness has in explaining things: things they themselves are confounded by. Had I had no community and no family on this journey—well, let me just say, let me just say, and let me just say again: I might not be here on this day. I love the ones who kept me alive—alive until the blue heron flies.

To the patient who suffers a mental illness, I know the difficulty of getting out of bed. Try and find a friend: find me, find community or even a pet you can tell anything to—and never stop searching for answers. God, I feel your pain, your confusion, your dismay at this point in your life, but it was written on every other page of this memoir—there is nothing wrong, but everything right with hope. Repeat these words, and keep on keeping on!

InfinitE/IQ, thus far, has given us strength and health with physical, mental and spiritual challenges, and a sense of community where dopamine is expelled, BDNF is released and night-filled, myelin-regenerating sleep ensures tomorrow to be my best day ever. If these are the gears of life, let clean fuel take the cog and run it smoothly— on and on.

Clean fuel embraces a macronutrient intake of proteins, carbohydrates and fats of the best kinds, and in the best proportion and ratio. The biochemistry and neurochemistry, and my personal experience, excitedly reports a feeling of energy and vibrancy. The science of satiation is in line with the concepts of seeking carbohydrates with low-glycemic indexes, joined with protein to stimulate glucagon and fat to drive cholecystokinin to fulfill the brain.

A plethora of exercise benefits have already been described, but physical training also curbs appetite. Understanding the glycemic index and portion control can actually leave all of us full, yet finding caloric restriction. The latter, of course, can have age-saving effects; we can all give our DNA a break. The wonders of clean fuel in controlling biochemistry are plentiful, including cortisol—a hormone of good or a hormone of harm.

And then we have long-chain fatty acids to further control a foundation of proto-hormone control. Take your EPA and DHA, eat clean fuel, walk out your door and devour life by embracing stimulation and community. The human body is a wondrous machine, equipped with sensors—modes of communication most will never understand—and back-up systems if trouble ensues. Clean fuel allows us to work with minimal stress, allowing our immune system to scavenge our bodies for danger, our vessels to flow unclogged, our bodies to walk lean without confounding chemistries, our joints to preserve hyaline cartilages, our inflammation to be minimized and our minds to function not in a haze—but with clarity and purpose.

InfinitE/IQ becomes, in of itself, a fulfilling way of life. Rolling with this System will bring positive experiences to further enhance life and well-being. Does the Traid prevent all bumps in the road? No, it does not. All of us understand life can be difficult at times. But *InfinitE/IQ* allows us to take a hit, learn from experiences and pave a new path forward. Bring others with you when you find a better road.

And so, I have written my last chapter before I head to the epilogue. The full, total solar eclipse of 2017 took a parabolic path from Oregon to Tennessee, so in New Jersey the moon was not able to totally block the sun. But, a member of my community—my church—sent a wonderful email to us all, telling of the remarkable corona he saw down south. In Tennessee, he witnessed the pulsing plasma amid a plummet of darkness, and sensed and was thankful for his shared joy. The moon has now traveled past the sun and our massive star shines again, and tomorrow morning I am left to a new day. Tomorrow is another dawn, a chance to write a few more words of conclusion and thanks and leave an opening for new life. The summer of 2017 has, indeed, left me free! I hope all of you are free too. I love you guys!

There is nothing wrong, but everything right with hope!

Epilogue

It is said the epilogue is reserved for works of fiction. This work by no means of that nature, but rather the story of truth and a call for examination and justice. I have written these words for you, the reader, and am so thankful for the absolute privilege and joy it has been to write for you: you have allowed me to be free. And so, allow me one last freedom, to use this wonderful Greek word *epi* in conclusion, and *logos* (the word, my words), to complete this memoir.

In 1978, I became ill. In 2009, I became well. The journey was long and arduous. I hope the historical analysis and science behind it will be of significant relevance for the patient. In this writing, I have done my best to adhere to *Patientes estote et venit Primus* (the Patient comes First).

In 2014, I created a website, and briefly explained my cure and reasons for it. I deleted those words out of concern for employment bias. At the same time, I began this book, the very early progress was halted again by that same concern. Two months ago, I had a meeting with a gentleman. At the end of the meeting, he told me to forget the bill for service and to finish the book. He inspired me, and I thank him. In took but a moment after that meeting, and the inspiration of my family, to propel forward and to pen away.

With the introduction of *InfinitE/IQ*, I proposed a means to mental and physical health, and suggested more scrutiny on the possibility of medication-induced side effects and sequelae. I do so with an understanding today's clinician has never been more strapped for time. It seems prudent that our healthcare system allow more billing time for difficult diagnoses. I believe if our healthcare system is to succeed, we need to educate better—and earlier—on the concepts of clean fuel and other benefits of my Formula. We need to offer a system of credits and debits, to reward those who take personal responsibility for their health, and make suggestions for those who don't.

Our education system needs to embrace early and continuous lessons on the human body, its systems, fuel requirements, how it adapts positively to challenges and the stresses to avoid. Our children require meals that maximize health, longevity and performance, and physical exercise to match the same goals.

InfinitE/IQ allowed me, nine plus years ago to find a lasting cure, and to find the moment and cherish it. It allowed me to embrace my wife and two children with endless love, and to seek community with others and stimulation from life. Without the aid of my father, mother and family, I cannot imagine surviving this thirty-one-year journey. You all saved my life. My girls never met you, Dad, but they ask often. I point on high, and tell proudly.

Two versions of *The Lindemann Theory, A 31 Year Journey and My Cure* were created, *For the World* and *For The Professional*. This was done so all 7+ billion on this planet could hear my message.

I hope this memoir opens eyes, advances medicine, raises questions and avoids such a journey for others. A pleasure it has been, and my final best wishes. Contact me anytime, reach out, if I can help in any way. *There is nothing wrong, but everything right with hope!*

With greatest sincerity, humility, caring and love, Robert W. Lindemann *Robert W. Lindemann*

REFERENCES

Truth be Told

Articles

"Facts & Statistics." American Association of Suicidology.

"Morbidity and Mortality Weekly Report (MMWR)." Centers for Disease Control and Prevention. October 01, 2010.

"NIH nearly doubles investment in BRAIN Initiative research." National Institutes of Health. October 14, 2016.

Introduction

Books

Blum, D. Love at Goon Park: Harry Harlow and the Science of Affection. Mass. Perseus, 2002.

Articles

King, James E., and Duane M. Rumbaugh. "Book Review Love at Goon Park: Harry Harlow and the Science of Affection by Deborah Blum." New England Journal of Medicine 348, no. 7 (2003): 670-71.

Chapter 3

Books

Craig, Charles R., and Robert E. Stitzel. Modern Pharmacology: Clinical Applications. Philadelphia, PA: Lippincott Williams & Wilkins, 1994.

Kandel, Eric R., Principles of Neural Science. NY, NY: McGraw-Hill Medical, 1991.

McGeer, Patrick L., John C. Eccles, and Edith G. McGeer. Molecular Neurobiology of the Mammalian Brain. New York: Plenum, 1987.

Chapter 6

Books

Kandel, Eric R., Principles of Neural Science. NY, NY: McGraw-Hill Medical, 1991.

McGeer, Patrick L., John C. Eccles, and Edith G. McGeer. Molecular Neurobiology of the Mammalian Brain. New York: Plenum, 1987.

Articles

Arnsten, Amy F. T., and Rebecca M. Shansky. "Adolescence: Vulnerable Period for Stress-Induced Prefrontal Cortical Function? Introduction to Part IV." Annals of the New York Academy of Sciences 1021, no. 1 (2004): 143-47.

Publishing, Harvard Health. "The Adolescent Brain: Beyond Raging Hormones." Harvard Health. Accessed November 21, 2017. https://www.health.harvard.edu/mind-and-mood/the-adolescent-brain-beyond-raging-hormones.

Casey BJ, et al. "Imaging the Developing Brain: What Have We Learned About Cognitive Development?" Trends in Cognitive Sciences. February 04, 2005.

GIEDD, JAY N. "Structural Magnetic Resonance Imaging of the Adolescent Brain." Annals of the New York Academy of Sciences. January 12, 2006.

Sisk, C. L., and D. L. Foster. "The Neural Basis of Puberty and Adolescence." Nature neuroscience. October 2004.

Steinberg, L. "Cognitive and Affective Development in Adolescence." Trends in cognitive sciences. February 2005.

Chapter 14

Books

Craig, Charles R., and Robert E. Stitzel. Modern Pharmacology:

Clinical Applications. Philadelphia, PA: Lippincott Williams & Wilkins, 1994.

Hall, John E., and Arthur C. Guyton. Guyton and Hall Textbook of Medical Physiology. Philadelphia, PA: Elsevier, 1986.

Articles

Gex-Fabry, Marianne, Androniki E. Balant-Gorgia, Luc P. Balant, and Gaston Garrone. "Clomipramine Metabolism." Clinical Pharmacokinetics 19, no. 3 (1990): 241-55.

Balant-Gorgia, Androniki E., Marianne Gex-Fabry, and Luc P. Balant. "Clinical Pharmacokinetics of Clomipramine." Clinical Pharmacokinetics 20, no. 6 (1991): 447-62.

Chapter 15

Books

Craig, Charles R., and Robert E. Stitzel. Modern Pharmacology: Clinical Applications. Philadelphia, PA: Lippincott Williams & Wilkins, 1994.

Hall, John E., and Arthur C. Guyton. Guyton and Hall Textbook of Medical Physiology. Philadelphia, PA: Elsevier, 1986.

Sears, B., The Zone. New York: Regan Books, 1995.

Articles

Toh, Hiroyuki, Atsushi Ichikawa, and Shuh Narumiya. "Molecular Evolution of Receptors for Eicosanoids." FEBS Letters 361, no. 1 (1995): 17-21.

Harizi, Hedi, Jean-Benoît Corcuff, and Norbert Gualde. "Arachidonic-acid-derived Eicosanoids: Roles in Biology and Immunopathology." Trends in Molecular Medicine 14, no. 10 (2008): 461-69.

Chapter 16

Books

McGeer, Patrick L., John C. Eccles, and Edith G. McGeer. Molecular Neurobiology of the Mammalian Brain. New York: Plenum, 1987.

Kandel, Eric R., Principles of Neural Science. NY, NY: McGraw-Hill Medical, 1991.

Hall, John E., and Arthur C. Guyton. Guyton and Hall Textbook of Medical Physiology. Philadelphia, PA: Elsevier, 1986.

McArdle, William D., Frank I. Katch, and Victor L. Katch. Exercise Physiology: Nutrition, Energy, and Human Performance. Baltimore: Wolters Kluwer Health/Lippincott Williams & Wilkins, 2007.

Baechle, Thomas R., and Roger W. Earle. Essentials of Strength Training and Conditioning. Champaign: Human Kinetics, 2000.

Exercise, American Council on. ACE Personal Trainer Manual Study Companion, 5th edition. American Council on Exercise, 1997.

Articles

Kastellakis, George, Denise J. Cai, Sara C. Mednick, Alcino J. Silva, and Panayiota Poirazi. "Synaptic Clustering Within Dendrites: An Emerging Theory of Memory Formation." Progress in Neurobiology 126 (2015): 19-35.

"Study Shows New Brain Connections Form Rapidly During Motor Learning." UC Santa Cruz News. https://news.ucsc.edu/2009/11/3413.html.

Chapter 17

Books

Craig, Charles R., and Robert E. Stitzel. Modern Pharmacology: Clinical Applications. Philadelphia, PA: Lippincott Williams & Wilkins, 1994.

McGeer, Patrick L., John C. Eccles, and Edith G. McGeer. Molecular Neurobiology of the Mammalian Brain. New York: Plenum, 1987.

Hall, John E., and Arthur C. Guyton. Guyton and Hall Textbook of Medical Physiology. Philadelphia, PA: Elsevier, 1986.

Kandel, Eric R., Principles of Neural Science. NY, NY: McGraw-Hill Medical, 1991.

Articles

Kim, Eun Joo, Blake Pellman, and Jeansok J. Kim. "Stress Effects on the Hippocampus: a Critical Review." Learning & Memory 22, no. 9 (2015): 411-16.

Fuchs, E., and G. Flügge. "Stress, Glucocorticoids and Structural Plasticity of the Hippocampus." Neuroscience & Biobehavioral Reviews 23, no. 2 (1998): 295-300.

Jacobson, Roni. "How Sleep Protects the Brain over Time." Scientific American Mind25, no. 1 (2013): 12.

Hara, Makoto R., Jeffrey J. Kovacs, Erin J. Whalen, Sudarshan Rajagopal, Ryan T. Strachan, Wayne Grant, Aaron J. Towers, Barbara Williams, Christopher M. Lam, Kunhong Xiao, Sudha K. Shenoy, Simon G. Gregory, Seungkirl Ahn, Derek R. Duckett, and Robert J. Lefkowitz. "A Stress Response Pathway Regulates DNA Damage Through β2-adrenoreceptors and β-arrestin-1." Nature 477, no. 7364 (2011): 349-53.

Chapter 19

Books

The Holy Bible. Dallas Texas: The Melton Book Company, 1971.

Baynes, John W., and Marek H. Dominiczak. Medical Biochemistry. Elsevier, 2014.

Friedman, P.J. Biochemistry. Boston. Little Brown and Company, 1995.

Craig, Charles R., and Robert E. Stitzel. Modern Pharmacology: Clinical Applications. Philadelphia, PA: Lippincott Williams & Wilkins, 1994.

Articles

Hara, Makoto R., Jeffrey J. Kovacs, Erin J. Whalen, Sudarshan Rajagopal, Ryan T. Strachan, Wayne Grant, Aaron J. Towers, Barbara Williams, Christopher M. Lam, Kunhong Xiao, Sudha K. Shenoy,

Simon G. Gregory, Seungkirl Ahn, Derek R. Duckett, and Robert J. Lefkowitz. "A Stress Response Pathway Regulates DNA Damage Through β2-adrenoreceptors and β-arrestin-1." Nature 477, no. 7364 (2011): 349-53.

Chapter 21

Books

McGeer, Patrick L., John C. Eccles, and Edith G. McGeer. Molecular Neurobiology of the Mammalian Brain. New York: Plenum, 1987.

Physician's Desk Reference 2016.

Craig, Charles R., and Robert E. Stitzel. Modern Pharmacology: Clinical Applications. Philadelphia, PA: Lippincott Williams & Wilkins, 1994.

Kandel, Eric R., Principles of Neural Science. NY, NY: McGraw-Hill Medical, 1991.

Articles

Kim, Eun Joo, Blake Pellman, and Jeansok J. Kim. "Stress Effects on the Hippocampus: a Critical Review." Learning & Memory 22, no. 9 (2015): 411-16.

Fuchs, E., and G. Flügge. "Stress, Glucocorticoids and Structural Plasticity of the Hippocampus." Neuroscience & Biobehavioral Reviews 23, no. 2 (1998): 295-300.

Hara, Makoto R., Jeffrey J. Kovacs, Erin J. Whalen, Sudarshan Rajagopal, Ryan T. Strachan, Wayne Grant, Aaron J. Towers, Barbara Williams, Christopher M. Lam, Kunhong Xiao, Sudha K. Shenoy, Simon G. Gregory, Seungkirl Ahn, Derek R. Duckett, and Robert J. Lefkowitz. "A Stress Response Pathway Regulates DNA Damage Through β2-adrenoreceptors and β-arrestin-1." Nature 477, no. 7364 (2011): 349-53.

Chapter 23

Books

West, G., Scale. New York: Penguin Press, 2017.

McGeer, Patrick L., John C. Eccles, and Edith G. McGeer. Molecular Neurobiology of the Mammalian Brain. New York: Plenum, 1987.

Sears, B. The Omega Rx Zone. New York: Regan Books, 2002.

Hall, John E., and Arthur C. Guyton. Guyton and Hall Textbook of Medical Physiology. Philadelphia, PA: Elsevier, 1986.

Articles

Rubin, D., and M. Laposata. "Cellular Interactions Between n-6 and n-3 Fatty Acids: a Mass Analysis of Fatty Acid Elongation/Desaturation, Distribution Among Complex Lipids, and Conversion to Eicosanoids." Journal of lipid research. October 1992.

Chapter 25

Books

McGeer, Patrick L., John C. Eccles, and Edith G. McGeer. Molecular Neurobiology of the Mammalian Brain. New York: Plenum, 1987.

Sears, B. The Omega Rx Zone. New York: Regan Books, 2002.

Hall, John E., and Arthur C. Guyton. Guyton and Hall Textbook of Medical Physiology. Philadelphia, PA: Elsevier, 1986.

Articles

Nigam, S. M., S. Xu, J. S. Kritikou, K. Marosi, L. Brodin, and M. P. Mattson. "Exercise and BDNF Reduce $A\beta$ Production by Enhancing α-secretase Processing of APP." Journal of Neurochemistry. July 2017.

Ferrer, I., E. Goutan, C. Marín, M. J. Rey, and T. Ribalta. "Brain-derived Neurotrophic Factor in Huntington Disease." Brain research. June 02, 2000.

Chapter 25

Books

McGeer, Patrick L., John C. Eccles, and Edith G. McGeer. Molecular Neurobiology of the Mammalian Brain. New York: Plenum, 1987.

Hall, John E., and Arthur C. Guyton. Guyton and Hall Textbook of Medical Physiology. Philadelphia, PA: Elsevier, 1986.

Kandel, Eric R., Principles of Neural Science. NY, NY: McGraw-Hill Medical, 1991.

Sears, B., The Zone. New York: Regan Books, 1995.

Articles

Chapter 28

Books

McGeer, Patrick L., John C. Eccles, and Edith G. McGeer. Molecular Neurobiology of the Mammalian Brain. New York: Plenum, 1987.

Hall, John E., and Arthur C. Guyton. Guyton and Hall Textbook of Medical Physiology. Philadelphia, PA: Elsevier, 1986.

Kandel, Eric R., Principles of Neural Science. NY, NY: McGraw-Hill Medical, 1991.

Sears, B., The Zone. New York: Regan Books, 1995.

Goodman, H.M. Basic Medical Endocrinology. New York: Raven Press, 1988.

Rosenfeld, Gary C., and David S. Loose-Mitchell. Pharmacology. Philadelphia: Wolters Kluwer Health/Lippincott Williams & Wilkins, 1993.

McArdle, William D., Frank I. Katch, and Victor L. Katch. Exercise Physiology: Nutrition, Energy, and Human Performance. Baltimore: Wolters Kluwer Health/Lippincott Williams & Wilkins, 2007.

Baechle, Thomas R., and Roger W. Earle. Essentials of Strength Training and Conditioning. Champaign: Human Kinetics, 2000.

Exercise, American Council on. ACE Personal Trainer Manual Study Companion, 5th Edition. American Council on Exercise, 1997.

Articles

Nigam, S. M., S. Xu, J. S. Kritikou, K. Marosi, L. Brodin, and M. P.

Mattson. "Exercise and BDNF Reduce Aβ Production by Enhancing α-secretase Processing of APP." Journal of neurochemistry. July 2017.

Ferrer, I., E. Goutan, C. Marín, M. J. Rey, and T. Ribalta. "Brain-derived Neurotrophic Factor in Huntington Disease." Brain research. June 02, 2000.

Rubin, D., and M. Laposata. "Cellular Interactions Between n-6 and n-3 Fatty Acids: a Mass Analysis of Fatty Acid Elongation/Desaturation, Distribution Among Complex Lipids, and Conversion to Eicosanoids." Journal of Lipid Research. October 1992.

Chapter 29

Books

Craig, Charles R., and Robert E. Stitzel. Modern Pharmacology: Clinical Applications. Philadelphia, PA: Lippincott Williams & Wilkins, 1994.

McArdle, William D., Frank I. Katch, and Victor L. Katch. Exercise Physiology: Nutrition, Energy, and Human Performance. Baltimore: Wolters Kluwer Health/Lippincott Williams & Wilkins, 2007.

Baechle, Thomas R., and Roger W. Earle. Essentials of Strength Training and Conditioning. Champaign: Human Kinetics, 2000.

Exercise, American Council on. ACE Personal Trainer Manual Study Companion, 5th Edition. American Council on Exercise, 1997.

Chapter 30

Books

Goodman, H.M. Basic Medical Endocrinology. New York: Raven Press, 1988.

Hall, John E., and Arthur C. Guyton. Guyton and Hall Textbook of Medical Physiology. Philadelphia, PA: Elsevier, 1986.

Chapter 31
Books

Sears, B., The Zone. New York: Regan Books, 1995.

Goodman, H.M. Basic Medical Endocrinology. New York: Raven Press, 1988.

Hall, John E., and Arthur C. Guyton. Guyton and Hall Textbook of Medical Physiology. Philadelphia, PA: Elsevier, 1986.

Articles

Talhout, Reinskje, Thomas Schulz, Ewa Florek, Jan Van Benthem, Piet Wester, and Antoon Opperhuizen. "Hazardous Compounds in Tobacco Smoke." International Journal of Environmental Research and Public Health. February 2011.

Chapter 32
Books

McGeer, Patrick L., John C. Eccles, and Edith G. McGeer. Molecular Neurobiology of the Mammalian Brain. New York: Plenum, 1987.

Hall, John E., and Arthur C. Guyton. Guyton and Hall Textbook of Medical Physiology. Philadelphia, PA: Elsevier, 1986.

Kandel, Eric R., Principles of Neural Science. NY, NY: McGraw-Hill Medical, 1991.

Sears, B., The Zone. New York: Regan Books, 1995.

Articles

Chapter 33
Books

McGeer, Patrick L., John C. Eccles, and Edith G. McGeer. Molecular Neurobiology of the Mammalian Brain. New York: Plenum, 1987.

Hall, John E., and Arthur C. Guyton. Guyton and Hall Textbook of Medical Physiology. Philadelphia, PA: Elsevier, 1986.

Kandel, Eric R., Principles of Neural Science. NY, NY: McGraw-Hill Medical, 1991.

Sears, B., The Zone. New York: Regan Books, 1995.

Sears, B. The Omega Rx Zone. New York: Regan Books, 2002.

Articles

Kim, Eun Joo, Blake Pellman, and Jeansok J. Kim. "Stress Effects on the Hippocampus: a Critical Review." Learning & Memory 22, no. 9 (2015): 411-16.

Fuchs, E., and G. Flügge. "Stress, Glucocorticoids and Structural Plasticity of the Hippocampus." Neuroscience & Biobehavioral Reviews 23, no. 2 (1998): 295-300.

Hara, Makoto R., Jeffrey J. Kovacs, Erin J. Whalen, Sudarshan Raja-gopal, Ryan T. Strachan, Wayne Grant, Aaron J. Towers, Barbara Williams, Christopher M. Lam, Kunhong Xiao, Sudha K. Shenoy, Simon G. Gregory, Seungkirl Ahn, Derek R. Duckett, and Robert J. Lefkowitz. "A Stress Response Pathway Regulates DNA Damage Through β2-adrenoreceptors and β-arrestin-1." Nature 477, no. 7364 (2011): 349-53.

Dyall, Simon C. "Long-chain Omega-3 Fatty Acids and the Brain: a Review of the Independent and Shared Effects of EPA, DPA and DHA." Frontiers in Aging Neuroscience 7 (2015).

Innis, Sheila M. "Dietary (n-3) Fatty Acids and Brain Develop-ment1,2." The Journal of Nutrition. April 01, 2007.

Chapter 34

Books

Craig, Charles R., and Robert E. Stitzel. Modern Pharmacology: Clinical Applications. Philadelphia, PA: Lippincott Williams & Wilkins, 1994.

McGeer, Patrick L., John C. Eccles, and Edith G. McGeer. Molecular Neurobiology of the Mammalian Brain. New York: Plenum, 1987.

Hall, John E., and Arthur C. Guyton. Guyton and Hall Textbook of Medical Physiology. Philadelphia, PA: Elsevier, 1986.

Kandel, Eric R., Principles of Neural Science. NY, NY: McGraw-Hill Medical, 1991.

Sears, B., The Zone. New York: Regan Books, 1995.

Chapter 35

Books

Craig, Charles R., and Robert E. Stitzel. Modern Pharmacology: Clinical Applications. Philadelphia, PA: Lippincott Williams & Wilkins, 1994.

McGeer, Patrick L., John C. Eccles, and Edith G. McGeer. Molecular Neurobiology of the Mammalian Brain. New York: Plenum, 1987.

Hall, John E., and Arthur C. Guyton. Guyton and Hall Textbook of Medical Physiology. Philadelphia, PA: Elsevier, 1986.

Kandel, Eric R., Principles of Neural Science. NY, NY: McGraw-Hill Medical, 1991.

Sears, B., The Zone. New York: Regan Books, 1995.

Articles

Kim, Eun Joo, Blake Pellman, and Jeansok J. Kim. "Stress Effects on the Hippocampus: a Critical Review." Learning & Memory 22, no. 9 (2015): 411-16.

Fuchs, E., and G. Flügge. "Stress, Glucocorticoids and Structural Plasticity of the Hippocampus." Neuroscience & Biobehavioral Reviews 23, no. 2 (1998): 295-300.

Hara, Makoto R., Jeffrey J. Kovacs, Erin J. Whalen, Sudarshan Rajagopal, Ryan T. Strachan, Wayne Grant, Aaron J. Towers, Barbara Williams, Christopher M. Lam, Kunhong Xiao, Sudha K. Shenoy, Simon G. Gregory, Seungkirl Ahn, Derek R. Duckett, and Robert J. Lefkowitz. "A Stress Response Pathway Regulates DNA Damage Through β2-adrenoreceptors and β-arrestin-1." Nature 477, no. 7364 (2011): 349-53.

Dyall, Simon C. "Long-chain Omega-3 Fatty Acids and the Brain: a

Review of the Independent and Shared Effects of EPA, DPA and DHA." Frontiers in Aging Neuroscience 7 (2015).

Innis, Sheila M. "Dietary (n-3) Fatty Acids and Brain Development1,2." The Journal of Nutrition. April 01, 2007.

Chapter 36

Books

Craig, Charles R., and Robert E. Stitzel. Modern Pharmacology: Clinical Applications. Philadelphia, PA: Lippincott Williams & Wilkins, 1994.

McGeer, Patrick L., John C. Eccles, and Edith G. McGeer. Molecular Neurobiology of the Mammalian Brain. New York: Plenum, 1987.

Hall, John E., and Arthur C. Guyton. Guyton and Hall Textbook of Medical Physiology. Philadelphia, PA: Elsevier, 1986.

Kandel, Eric R., Principles of Neural Science. NY, NY: McGraw-Hill Medical, 1991.

Sears, B., The Zone. New York: Regan Books, 1995.

West, G., Scale. New York: Penguin Press, 2017.

McArdle, William D., Frank I. Katch, and Victor L. Katch. Exercise Physiology: Nutrition, Energy, and Human Performance. Baltimore: Wolters Kluwer Health/Lippincott Williams & Wilkins, 2007.

Baechle, Thomas R., and Roger W. Earle. Essentials of Strength Training and Conditioning. Champaign: Human Kinetics, 2000.

Exercise, American Council on. ACE Personal Trainer Manual Study Companion, 5th edition. American Council on Exercise, 1997.

Heine, S.J., DNA Is Not Destiny. New York: W.W. Norton and Company, Inc., 2017.

Blum, D. Love at Goon Park: Harry Harlow and the Science of Affection. Mass. Perseus, 2002.

Articles

Kim, Eun Joo, Blake Pellman, and Jeansok J. Kim. "Stress Effects on the Hippocampus: a Critical Review." Learning & Memory 22, no. 9 (2015): 411-16.

Fuchs, E., and G. Flügge. "Stress, Glucocorticoids and Structural Plasticity of the Hippocampus." Neuroscience & Biobehavioral Reviews 23, no. 2 (1998): 295-300.

Hara, Makoto R., Jeffrey J. Kovacs, Erin J. Whalen, Sudarshan Rajagopal, Ryan T. Strachan, Wayne Grant, Aaron J. Towers, Barbara Williams, Christopher M. Lam, Kunhong Xiao, Sudha K. Shenoy, Simon G. Gregory, Seungkirl Ahn, Derek R. Duckett, and Robert J. Lefkowitz. "A Stress Response Pathway Regulates DNA Damage Through β2-adrenoreceptors and β-arrestin-1." Nature 477, no. 7364 (2011): 349-53.

Dyall, Simon C. "Long-chain Omega-3 Fatty Acids and the Brain: a Review of the Independent and Shared Effects of EPA, DPA and DHA." Frontiers in Aging Neuroscience 7 (2015).

Innis, Sheila M. "Dietary (n-3) Fatty Acids and Brain Development1,2." The Journal of Nutrition. April 01, 2007.

King, James E., and Duane M. Rumbaugh. "Book Review Love at Goon Park: Harry Harlow and the Science of Affection by Deborah Blum." New England Journal of Medicine 348, no. 7 (2003): 670-71.

Acknowledgements

Fulfillment of The Lindemann Theory, will require a passionate grasping of the components of InfinitE/IQ: Community, Stimulation (mental and physical) and Clean Fuel.

Bringing the words from my fingertips to the marketplace required a micro-journey in itself and entrance to/satisfaction of some of those three components – community and mental/creative stimulation. It involved interacting with some very wonderful people.

I can only compare the experience to a recent viewing of a rare meteorological event of twin water spouts spiraling in concert across a vast body of water – separate entities –then interacting – separate – and find completion as one funnel – a whole. The one hundred plus mph funnel speed brings to mind dendritic lightening, the exchange of ideas, and then fruition of a product.

With such noted, much gratitude to the following people:

To my parents, family, and caregivers a tearful embrace for keeping me alive, until my 2009 epiphany which brought an 8 plus year cure to reality.

To my wife and wonderful two children, the love and joy is abundant, and drives me forward at every dawn, and blessed at every rest.

To my teachers and professors that equipped me with knowledge, enabling me to analyze, and find resolve – much thanks.

To my community, friends and church, the support has been bounteous.

The following people, in first name alphabetical order all contributed with feedback of inspiring words for this project:

Bai Lor	Pastor David Jahnke
Bill Lindemann	Pastor Rob Cruver
Bob Marotto	Rhaena Lindemann
Charles McCormack	Richard Gearhart
Claire Lindemann	Rochelle Lindemann
Craig Lindemann	Rosanne Lindemann
David Lindemann	Tom Kimball

A special thanks to the staff at Graham Communications, involved with the editing, and formatting of this book. A huge thank you is given to Pat Pfleger for book cover design in a joint venture with Robert Lindemann and to Gregory Heh from Jersey Printing for introducing me to Pat. Much gratitude is extended to Richard Gearhart, and the staff at Gearhart Law. In addition, a huge thanks to Mike Beach and Mike LaSalle, from Parker Banks Video Production for a complimentary video book announcement. That referral coming from Mary Demont of Barbizon of Red Bank - a huge thanks. In final, much appreciation to Bai Lor for web site design and development.

ABOUT THE AUTHOR

ROBERT LINDEMANN is the author and publisher of The Lindemann Theory, A 31 Year Journey and My Cure. His 31 years of practical medical psychology, atop a profound educational and research experience in physiology, sports physiology, psychology and training has enabled this cure and its sharing. He lives in the garden state of New Jersey with his wife and two daughters. Visit the author's website at http://www.thelindemanntheory.com.

www.ingramcontent.com/pod-product-compliance
Lightning Source LLC
Chambersburg PA
CBHW052033090426
42739CB00010B/1895